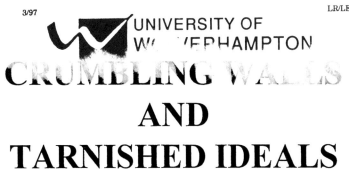

UNIVERSITY OF
WOLVERHAMPTON

CRUMBLING WALLS
AND
TARNISHED IDEALS

An Ethnography of East Germany
Before and After Unification

Hans Baer   ae 306.209431

University Press of America,® Inc.
Lanham • New York • Oxford

Copyright © 1998 by
University Press of America,® Inc.
4720 Boston Way
Lanham, Maryland 20706

12 Hid's Copse Rd.
Cummor Hill, Oxford OX2 9JJ

Library of Congress Cataloging-in-Publication Data

Baer, Hans A.
Crumbling walls and tarnished ideals : an ethnography of East
Germany before and after unification / Hans Baer.
p.   cm.
Includes bibliographical references and index.
1. Political culture—Germany (East). 2. Historiography—Germany
(East). 3. Germany (East)—Politics and government. 4.
Dissenters—Germany (East). 5. Germany—History—Unification,
1990. 6. Germany—History—1990-   I. Title.
DD289.B32   1998   932'.1087 —DC21   97-49283 CIP

ISBN 0-7618-1020-X (cloth: alk. ppr.)

Contents

Tables and Figures

Acknowledgements

Numerous sources of support in terms of both time and funds made it possible for me to gather the materials and insights that contributed to the writing of this book. A grant from the GDR-USA Friendship Society made it possible for me to attend a summer course during 18 June - 9 August, 1988, on "Social Life in the German Democratic Republic" at the teachers' college in Erfurt. Grants from the Council for International Exchange of Scholars and Humboldt University allowed me to spend the period between early September 1988 and late February 1989 as a Fulbright Lecturer in the Department of British and American Studies at Humboldt University in East Berlin. A grant from the National Endowment for the Humanities permitted me to attend the seminar on "Democratizing Leninist States" (directed by Edward Friedman) at the University of Wisconsin-Madison during the period 18 June to 9 August, 1990. A small grant from the Office of Research and Sponsored Programs at the University of Arkansas at Little Rock provided me with support to conduct ethnographic research in the new German states while on sabbatical in Spring semester 1991. A joint grant from the Fulbright Commission of Germany and the Council for International Exchange of Scholars permitted me to attend a traveling seminar on the unification process during the period 22 June to 24 July 1991. A grant from the German Academic Exchange Service allowed me to attend a seminar on "United Germany in a Modern World" (co-directed by Ellen Kennedy and Frank Trommler) at the University of Pennsylvania during the period 15 June to 16 July, 1992. A grant from the National Endowment for the Humanities allowed me to attend the seminar on "Rethinking European History, 1945-1989" (directed by Tony Judt) at New York University during the period of 21 June to 4 August, 1993. Funding from the Life and Peace Institute in Uppsala, Sweden, provided me with the opportunity to revisit East Germany during summer 1995. Although my observations on the sociopolitical status of the East German churches will be published in a forthcoming Institute volume, I was able to visit various friends and acquaintances whose experiences and perceptions are reported in this book.

Kluwer Academic Publishers gave me permission to incorporate portions of two articles that I published in *Dialectical Anthropology* in this book. The articles are "The Legitimation Crisis in the German Democratic

Republic Before the Opening of the Wall: Views from Below" [Vol. 17(1992):319-337] and "Conversations with Two Former Socialist Unity Party Members: Views of Life in East Germany" [Vol. 20(1995):387-412]. I appreciate comments that Stella Capek, Merrill Singer, Michael Kleine, and Tony Judt made in their reading of earlier drafts of my book manuscript. Finally, I appreciate the technical support and copy-editing that Beth Houck performed in the preparation of this book.

Introduction

Many Westerners depicted the former German Democratic Republic (GDR) before the opening of the Wall in November 1989 as a police state ruled by a Stalinist Communist party which imposed totalitarian controls upon a people who would have rather lived in the real democratic Germany, namely the Federal Republic of Germany (FRG). On the negative side, Western views of the GDR conjured up images of a Wall that separated East Berlin from West Berlin, an "Iron Curtain" that separated the two Germanies, and cities and towns filled with drab buildings and depressed people who enviously hungered for the consumer products readily available in the other Germany and who would have fled from their miserable living conditions if they had the opportunity to do so. On the positive side, Westerners thought of the GDR's successes in the Olympics (in which it placed second only to the Soviet Union and ahead of the United States) and Katrina Witt, the world-famous ice skating champion who since the German unification has sought additional fame and fortune in the capitalist West.

Liberal scholars, who presented a more sophisticated view of GDR society, tended to view it as the staunchest ally of the Soviet Union (Childs 1983). Even progressive scholars often depicted the GDR as a society of a "frozen revolution" (1982). Most scholarly accounts of the GDR focused on the inner workings of the Socialist Unity Party of Germany (SED or *Sozialistische Einheitspartei Deutschlands*), the relationship between the GDR state and the Soviet Union, other Eastern European states, and capitalist states, particularly the FRG; and an economic system that had produced the highest material standard of living in the Eastern bloc, while ignoring the realities of every-day life in the GDR (Ludz 1970, 1972; Baylis 1974; McCauley 1979, 1983; Scharf 1984).

Stereotypes, both real and scholarly, often contain an element of truth, but basically they make exaggerated and distorted statements about social reality. This observation applies no less to depictions of East German society, which in large part were based upon brief trips to the GDR and attempts to read between the lines of GDR state publications and official statements. In this book, I attempt to present a corrective to Western conventional portrayals of East German society, both before and after unification, based largely upon data obtained through participant-observation in the former GDR and the new East German states of the FRG. In addition to relying upon my own observations, I attempt to provide an account of social life in East Germany before and after the unification through the eyes of ordinary East Germans from various backgrounds.

As a critical anthropologist, I have been interested for some time in the ideals and realities of socialism. As part of this interest, I have been engaged in an independent reading project on the nature of post-revolutionary societies for two interrelated reasons, one theoretical and the other political. At the theoretical level, I have been interested in the question as to whether post-revolutionary societies are examples of state socialism or "actually existing socialism," state capitalism, transitions between capitalism and socialism, or new class formations. An even more significant issue for me, however, is why did discrepancies develop between the ideals of socialism and the realities of these societies, aside of how they are defined? As I explain later in this book, I tend to view post-revolutionary societies as transitions between capitalism and socialism which require a process of political democratization if they are to evolve into authentically socialist societies. From my perspective, such a development is not inevitable but is necessary to ensure social equity and justice to the people of the world and to live in harmony with a fragile ecosystem which the capitalist productivist ethic threatens to destroy. As part of my commitment to in some way being part of the complex process of creating a more just world system, I wanted to witness social life in a post-revolutionary society first-hand and, in doing so, gain insights into the discrepancies between the ideals and realities of socialism.

With this thought in mind, I applied twice for a Fulbright Lectureship in the Soviet Union. Both in 1986 and 1987 I was one of 35 Americans nominated for a Fulbright Scholarship in the Soviet Union. I had even received a stipend from the Council for International Exchange of Scholars (CIES) to study beginning Russian in an eight week intensive language course at Bryn Mawr College.

Much to my disappointment, I was not one of the 15 Americans who were selected by the Soviet Ministry of Education in 1986 and 1987 for Fulbright Scholarships. Paul Hiemstra at CIES advised me to apply for a Fulbright lectureship in the German Democratic Republic and to prepare a course syllabus in American studies because there was great interest in this topic in the GDR. Much to my delight, the Department of British and American Studies at Humboldt University in East Berlin accepted my proposal to teach on "The Anthropology and Sociology of American Society" during the 1988-1989 academic year. I was part of the second delegation of Fulbright Scholars to visit the GDR. Even if I did not receive a Fulbright Scholarship, I was determined to visit the GDR and received a stipend from the GDR-USA Friendship Society to attend a course on "Social Life in the German Democratic Republic" at the teachers' college in Erfurt, a beautiful medieval city of some 250,000 residents in the heart of Thuringia between 28 July and 19 August 1988.

I also had personal reasons for wanting to visit the GDR. Part of my family roots lie in East Germany. My father was born in 1901 in Berlin and my mother was born in 1905 in Burg, a small city east of Magdeburg. In 1929 my father accepted a three year contract with a German company to work in Peru. When his contract ended, he decided to find other employment in Peru because he feared that he would not be able to find a job in Germany which by this time was in the midst of the Great Depression. My mother left Germany in 1933, shortly after Hitler had come to power, in order to marry my father and start a new life in a distant land. Both my brother and I were born in Lima, Peru - I on 6 April 1944, and he on 22 September 1946. In 1949 my father immigrated a second time, this time to the United States. My mother, brother, and I rejoined him on 1 January 1951, in New York Harbor after a long ocean voyage. Unfortunately, my parents for complex reasons never returned to Germany, even for a visit. I did not meet any of my relatives until July 1969 when I visited my father's brother, his wife, their two daughters, my paternal grandmother, who passed away at the age of 93 years a few years later, in the small city of Bruchsal situated between Heidelberg and Karlsruhe in West Germany. When I visited my uncle, aunt, and cousins again in May 1983 prior to conducting ethnographic and archival research on osteopathy and chiropractic in Great Britain, I told one of my cousins that I had grown up in large part without a family history, at least in the form that most children do with at least periodic direct contact with relatives. While I had occasionally visited some of my West German relatives, I had never visited any of my East German relatives, all of whom are on my mother's side of the family. My visits to East Germany during 1988-1989 and in 1991 allowed me to establish contact with some of these relatives as well as with some of my relatives on my father's side of the family who reside in West Berlin.

Mine is the third book on East Germany written by former Fulbright Scholar. Peter Marcuse, a professor of architecture at Columbia University, wrote a book on his experiences in the GDR during the 1989-1990 academic year while a Fulbright Scholar at the Bauhaus in

Weimar and later in Berlin. Although the German version of his book carries the English title of *A German Way of Revolution*, it was translated into German and essentially is a daily journal of his experiences in the GDR during a time that closely corresponds with the period called *die Wende* (the turn) which involved the opening of the Wall, the resignation of the Politburo, the free elections of March 1990, and the currency union of July 1990 (Marcuse 1990a). Marcuse's (1991) account more recently appeared in English and includes an assessment of the impact of the political merger of the two Germanies upon social life in East Germany. Paul Gleye (1991), an associate professor of architecture at Montana State University, has written an impressionistic account of his experiences in the GDR while he was a lecturer at the *Hochschule fuer Architectikur und Bauwesen* (HAB or College of Architecture and Building Design) -- better known as the *Bauhaus* in Weimar during the 1988-1989. While I did not become well acquainted with Paul, we occasionally spoke with one another at various events in East Berlin to which Fulbright Scholars had been invited. While my book also includes impressions based upon my experiences in the GDR - ones that undoubtedly paralleled those of Marcuse and Gleye but also differed, it also includes a social scientific analysis of the legitimation crisis that existed in the last days of the GDR and both an account and an analysis of social life in East Germany after the political merger of the GDR and the FRG.

In some ways, my book should complement anthropologist John Borneman's (1991) recent ethnographic study which portrays the experiences of individual East Berliners during the last years of the GDR, the Wende, and up to May 1990 by which time it became clear that a rapid political merger of the two Germanies or, more accurately, an absorption of the GDR by the FRG would occur. Like Borneman, although less from an interpretative or phenomenological perspective and more from a critical anthropological perspective that attempts to make macro-micro connections between the capitalist world-system and the local context in which anthropologists generally conduct their fieldwork, I examine different voices from East Germany as they reflect upon life in the former German Democratic Republic and grapple with the complexities of life as second-class citizens in the new Germany.

Like virtually all East Germans as well as scholars both in the West and East, I assumed that the German Democratic Republic would continue to exist for some time to come. With this thought in mind, I began to contemplate the possibility of becoming a "GDR specialist" during my stay in the GDR. In a sense, my new-found specialty disappeared with the political merger of the two Germanies. Also, the

GDR would no longer serve as a living case study for research on post-revolutionary or socialist-oriented societies. While prior to the unification, most Western scholars regarded the GDR to be part of Eastern Europe, the political merger precluded easily marshaling it into the same category as other Eastern European societies, such as Czechoslovakia, Poland, Hungary, and Yugoslavia. It is not even clear how to refer to the territory of the former GDR. In the new Germany, it is now generally referred to as *die neue Bundeslaender* (the new German states consisting of Brandenburg, Saxony, Saxony-Anhalt, Thuringia, Mecklenberg-Vorpommern and united Berlin). One can, of course, speak of western Germany and eastern Germany in referring to the "old German states" and the "new German states." Nevertheless, "West Germany" and "East Germany" continue to exist and will probably continue to exist for some time as sociological entities. In some ways, this is analogous to speaking of the "North" and the "South" in the United States, despite the fact that the Confederate States of America were reincorporated into the United States of America. Just as the Union never recognized the Confederacy as a legitimate nation-state, the FRG never granted official diplomatic recognition to the GDR, even though the former eventually came to develop a number of political, economic, and cultural ties with the latter. Given that all of the countries in Eastern Europe are in a state of flux, one may make the case that sociologically-speaking East Germany remains in a number of ways a part of Eastern Europe.

At any rate, John Cole (1985:240-242) maintains that the following characteristics of critical anthropology enable American anthropologists to "contribute something distinctive to the critical discourse on Eastern Europe": (1) participant-observation as its principal research strategy; (2) "non-corporate" or "informal" social relations with members of the host society; (3) qualitative research; (4) the study of a particular community, institution, or process within its larger context; and (5) the examination of "social and cultural practice as it affects the human condition." By adopting these research strategies during the course of my extended stay in the GDR in 1988-1989, I was able to obtain a first-hand glimpse of every-day life in a post-revolutionary society, one which neither I nor any East German with whom I spoke apparently suspected would be within the next year or so propelled toward the Wende, a complex process that would culminate in political merger with or absorption by the FRG. In addition to contacts with faculty members, staff, and students at Humboldt University and other GDR universities and colleges, I established contacts with GDR citizens from many walks of life, including school teachers, engineers, economists, physicians, state functionaries, factory workers, church leaders, as well as many rank-and-file members of the Socialist Unity Party of Germany (SED). My interactions with some of these people occurred frequently and even developed into what I hope will prove to be long-term friendships. Indeed, when I returned to East Germany on two occasions in 1991, I reestablished contact with many of the people who I had met in the GDR. Furthermore, I came into contact with many more East Germans during my visits in 1991. It is through the eyes of these East Germans coupled with my own theoretical perspective as a critical anthropologist that I present an ethnography of political change in East Germany before and after unification.

In the first chapter, I present a personal account of my initial impressions of the GDR, my experiences as a Fulbright Lecturer at Humboldt University, and my adventures as an *Ami* (the German nickname for an American) in East Berlin and the GDR.

In Chapter 2, based upon conversations and interviews with East Germans from various walks of life, I examine the "legitimation crisis" in the GDR before the opening of the Wall. I discuss the views of East Germans on SED elites and state functionaries, the GDR economy, the media, and the ideals and realities of socialism, and their responses to glasnost and perestroika. Whereas my subjects saw major contradictions in GDR society, most of them continued to subscribe to the ideals of socialism. Unlike in many other East European countries, "socialism" had not become a dirty word.

Chapter 3 argues that the GDR prior to the opening of the Wall constituted a neo-Stalinist state antithetical to the notion of socialist democracy. While the GDR constitution formally provided for democratic processes in the polity, the work place, and social life, the monopoly of power exercised by SED elites precluded expression of these ideals in the GDR. A question of greater importance than the actual nature of the GDR is that of why an authoritarian state continued to exist in the GDR, even after the death of Stalin in 1953, and after it evolved into a relatively, but by no means fully, developed industrial society. In attempting to answer this question, I examine several external and internal factors that shaped the development of the Soviet Zone and what in 1949 became the GDR.

Whereas most studies of the SED view it from above, Chapter 4 views it from below by focusing on the experiences of several former SED members in rank-and-file and lower-echelon leadership positions. The experiences suggest that at least some SED members attempted in various ways to reform the Party, but were thwarted by a bureaucratic structure that stifled dissent from below. These former SED members explore the ideals and realities of socialism as it existed in the GDR and the reasons that the GDR state collapsed.

Chapter 5 presents my own personal observations of social life in the new German states or East Germany in the months following the political merger of the two Germanys in December 1990. These occurred initially during the period of January 31 - April 7, 1991, while I spent part of my sabbatical in East Germany and again in July 1991 as a part of a seminar on the "German Unification" sponsored by the Fulbright Commission in Bonn, Schleswig-Holstein, Mecklenberg-Vorpommern, and Berlin.

Chapter 6 discusses the perceptions of social life in the new Germany held by three categories of East Germans-former SED professionals, non-SED professionals, and workers, some of whom belonged to the SED but most of whom did not - with whom I conducted intensive interviews in early 1991.

In Chapter 7, I examine the status of the opposition consisting of Alliance (*Buendnis*) 90, the United Left, and the Party of Democratic Socialism (PDS or the reconstituted SED) in the new German states as expressed through the voices of some of their participants. The grass-roots movement that played an instrumental role during the Wende had a different conception of what the future of the GDR should be than that of the East German masses. In this chapter, I also discuss the efforts of PDS to come to grips with its SED past and to function as a partner of the political opposition, one that is by and large distrusted by the grass-roots groups.

The concluding chapter assesses the contradictions of the forty year history of the GDR, not only its shortcomings but also its achievements. It attempts to analyze the collapse of the GDR in the context of the demise of Stalinism in the Soviet Union and Eastern Union. Did the collapse of the GDR serve as one more example that capitalism is the end of history or may it provide the space by which democratic socialist ideals eventually may blossom as East Germans come to grips with the realities of their second-class citizenship in the new Germany?

Chapter 1

A Fulbright Scholar's Experiences in the GDR

This chapter provides a journalistic account of my initial impressions of the German Democratic Republic, my experiences as a Fulbright Lecturer at Humboldt University in East Berlin and at other institutions in the GDR, and my travels around the various cities and regions of that country.

Initial Impressions of the GDR

I entered the GDR for the first time en route by train from Frankfurt am Main to Erfurt on 28 July, 1991. Given the horror stories that one hears about border crossings into Eastern Europe, I was prepared to empty the contents of my backpack which contained my personal belongings, other than most of my books which had been forwarded by mail to the U.S. Embassy in East Berlin. Much to my surprise, I found the demeanor of the GDR border guards who entered the train for their customary inspection at Gerlungen to be relatively easygoing. Ironically, the most frightening border crossing that I have ever made was not into a foreign country, including Mexico on numerous occasions, Guatemala in 1982, and Czechoslovakia in 1989, but into the United States upon a return trip from Mexico and Guatemala in the summer of 1982. Perhaps the U.S. customs officials at the Dallas/Fort Worth International Airport interpreted my beard and backpack as the signs that I might be a drug smuggler. Although I knew that I had no drugs in my possession or that I had not committed a crime, my heart pounded heavily when I was asked to go into a small room where the contents of my backpack were inspected. Like never before or afterwards, I felt the might of the U.S. government penetrate my body and mind. I literally became transformed into what Scheper-Hughes and Lock (1987) term the "mindful body." Perhaps the GDR border guards interpreted the presence of two visas, both of which were *Gebuehrenfrei* (duty-free), for the periods 28 July - 20 August, 1988, and 1 September 1988 - 28 February 1989, respectively, to mean that I was a guest of the GDR state and therefore be treated differently than a tourist. Indeed, at no time in my border crossings between the FRG and the GDR and between West Berlin and East Berlin were the contents of my baggage inspected.

The remainder of my train trip revealed a landscape filled with rusty, dilapidated, and shoddy factories, railroad equipment, train stations, and apartment buildings that in some ways reminded me more of what one views from a train ride on the Northeast corridor and the Midwestern "Rustbelt" of the United States than the tidy and prosperous appearance of West Germany. Conversely, many of the farm houses that the train passed appeared substantial, even if most of them lacked the well-painted look of their West German counterparts. While much of the central business district of Erfurt struck me as picturesque and well-preserved, the *Neubau* (new construction) apartments in the vicinity of the student dormitory where I was to spend the next three weeks struck me as sterile in their functionality. In viewing such Neubau areas which exist throughout East Germany, I often asked myself, "Is this what has happened to the socialist dream?" While many East Germans preferred to reside in these areas because the apartments in them had central heating whereas those in the older areas did not, they also had a reaction not too different from mine to them.

As I observed people scurrying in and out of stores in Erfurt, I quickly came to the conclusion that the GDR also was a consumer society, even if the stores did not carry the variety and the quality of goods that their counterparts in the West do. Aside of the material aspects of life, an incident that occurred on my second day Erfurt suggested to me that East Germans felt safer in their surroundings than did Americans. As I was sitting in the plaza outside of the main train station in Erfurt, a little girl asked me for a piece of cake. When her mother saw her eating the cake that I had given her, she amusedly scolded her for begging and the older man with them laughed. I suspect that most American parents have socialized their children never to request anything from a stranger and certainly not to accept something from one. Furthermore, I imagined that I would never have given a little girl in my own country a piece of cake, even upon request in the presence of a parent, in order to avoid the possibility of being accused of attempting to molest the child. My first two days in Erfurt, which I had pretty much to myself, demonstrated to me that the GDR indeed was a country of contradictions.

The course that I attended on "Social Life in the GDR" was one of several courses on German language and culture offered at institutions of higher learning by the League for People's Friendship (*Liga fuer Voelkerfreundship*), a state propaganda organ similar in some ways to the United States Information Agency (USIA). At the opening meeting of the four classes in our session of the summer program, the female rector of the teachers' college in Erfurt told us that the some 130 participants present came from four continents and 22 countries. She expressed the hope that the GDR would become a "nuclear-free zone" in order to ensure that another war would never occur on German soil. Whereas the students in our session all came from capitalist countries, students from various East European countries also attended courses at the same time at the college but were housed in a separate dormitory, apparently in order to minimize interaction between the two groups. Nevertheless, it was possible to mingle with the Eastern Europeans in the pub in the student union. On one occasion they sang "Happy Birthday" to one of their colleagues in English rather than in Russian, perhaps a subtle indicator of their antipathy toward the Soviet Union.

Even though the purpose of our summer course was to present the GDR in a favorable light, the director and his two female assistants were quite willing to handle critical questions about their society. One of our guest lecturers admitted that the construction of socialism had been more difficult than many had anticipated. In our concluding session, the director of our course told us that he and his colleagues had attempted to present the GDR as it really existed, not any better or worse. He also solicited our impressions about our observations of social life in the GDR.

In addition to lectures and seminars, the summer course included cultural performances and field trips, such as ones to Buchenwald (a former Nazi concentration camp), Weimar, a Kindergarten, a senior citizen's recreational center, and a Young Pioneers camp. Our tour guide at a camp called *Pioneer Lager Maxim Gorki* near Eisenach told us that parents paid only eight *Ostmarks* (Eastmarks) for their children to stay in the camp for two weeks. Teachers accompanied their pupils to the camp where the latter received four hours of instruction in the mornings.

Our group also visited an electronics firm with about 2,100 employees. A sign outside the plant proclaimed, "High achievements for the prosperity of the people and peace - Everything for the actualization of the resolutions of the Eleventh SED Congress." Apparently such slogans were largely ineffective in motivating employees to work harder. One of our student assistants told me that during her stint as a student worker in a factory, she discovered that she was the only one in her group working hard and that her fellow workers took frequent breaks. Indeed, the director of one of the plant sections admitted that some workers exhibit a pattern of absenteeism and others don't exert themselves. He noted that no one was denied employment in the GDR and that workers can receive up to six weeks of sick leave at 90 percent of their wages. The plant had a four-year apprenticeship for Cuban workers who also received German language training. In addition to Cubans, the GDR also had many Vietnamese, Mozambican, and Angolan apprentices working in its factories. Although pornography was officially banned in the GDR, some of the employees had pin-ups of scantily clad women, which had come to be accepted by the state as "art," at their work stations. Much of the more modern equipment in the plant had been manufactured in the FRG. The director of the summer program told us that it was quite difficult arranging a visit to a factory in the GDR.

Participants in the summer program were given a considerable amount of time to explore the GDR on their own. The most memorable event for me occurred on a side-trip to the mountain resort village of Oberhof with a Cypriot English teacher who also spoke German and Russian. As we were sitting at an outdoors fast-food eatery (*Imbiss*), three Soviet officers and their driver joined us at our table. The only one of the officers who spoke German asked us our place of origin. When the officers learned that I am an American, they purchased two brandies and later a round of beers for my friend and me. One of the officers joked about the American drinking with "Communists" and we all toasted to peace, friendship, and our common humanity. I had difficulty imagining three American officers engaging in a similar ritual with a Soviet citizen. One of the officers, a 34 year old lieutenant from the Ukraine, gave a long speech in Russian while one of his colleagues translated it into fluent German. Given that I had already drunk a large glass of beer and only eaten a small sausage before the arrival of the Soviet military entourage, I found the entire proceeding surrealistic as my head spun from the combination of brandy and beer on a relatively empty stomach. At one point when I could no longer hold my bladder, I thought that I might collapse on my way to the rest room but fortunately I managed to successfully negotiate my way.

After visiting relatives for a week and a half in West Germany, I arrived in West Berlin on the evening of September 1. I had received instructions from the United States Information Agency, the branch of the

State Department that funds the Fulbright Program, to disembark at the Zoo train station in the hectic Ku'Damm - the commercial center of West Berlin - where I was to be met by a driver from the U.S. Embassy in East Berlin. Unfortunately, somehow we missed each other. After calling the embassy, I was instructed to take a bus to Checkpoint Charlie where Peter Claussen, the Cultural Attache, met me. As I awaited my driver, who had reported in that he had not found me at the train station, I had a surrealistic sense of time and space as I stood at what perhaps constituted the most poignant symbol of the Cold War.

My East German driver took me to my assigned apartment at Karl Maron Strasse 2 in Marzahn, the oldest Neubau area in East Berlin, where I was met by an *Assistant* (assistant professor) from the Department of British and American Studies at Humboldt University. Somehow the Office of International Relations at the university was under the impression that my two children would be staying with me and assigned me an apartment with a living room, kitchen, and two bedrooms. Since I was aware of the housing shortage in the GDR and did not feel need for such a spacious area for merely myself, I moved about a week later to an efficiency apartment. The university rented apartments on the fourth, fifth, and sixth floors to visiting faculty members and students. Although an unfurnished efficiency apartment, along with utilities, such as mine would have cost a GDR citizen about 50 Marks, I was charged 252 Marks. In part, this may have been a way of covering the expenses for the furniture, black and white television, radio, small washing machine, dishware, and utensils in my apartment.

At any rate, in addition to the half salary that the University of Arkansas at Little Rock and the stipend that CIES gave me, I received a monthly salary of 1,800 Marks and a "start-up" stipend of 1,500 Marks from the university. Never in my entire life had I had so much disposable income. Since the money that I received from the university was non-convertible currency, even after buying gifts for significant others at home and books, records, and several sweaters for myself, I had so much money that I was able to often treat my friends and students to food and drinks at restaurants and cafes, something which I could not afford to do as a regular practice in the United States. My next door neighbors at Karl Maron Strasse were Robert and Tamara Geiger. Robert grew up in the Ukraine as the child of a German Catholic father and Mennonite mother. Tamara is Russian and has only a rudimentary knowledge of German. Robert was a visiting professor in the Department of Slavic Languages at Humboldt University and Tamara taught Russian at the Pioneer Palace in East Berlin.

The View from the Campus: Teaching in the GDR

Perhaps because my academic career as both a student and a faculty member has been for the most part at non-elite institutions, it was somewhat difficult for me to accept that as a Fulbright Lecturer at Humboldt University I was teaching at one of Europe's most famous universities. Wilhelm von Humboldt, a famous German educator, founded the Berlin University, which was renamed Humboldt University after World War II, in 1809 as a center of scholarship and research. Many famous scholars, including Georg Hegel, Rudolf Virchow, Aldoph Bastien, Max Planck, and Albert Einstein, had taught at the University. Although Karl Marx eventually obtained his doctorate at Jena University, most of his university education, including under the influence of the young Hegelians, had occurred at this institution. Franz Boas, who is still regarded by many as the most important figure in American anthropology, studied physics and geography at Berlin University and W.E.B. DuBois, the famous African-American sociologist, historian, social activist, and journalist, conducted postdoctoral studies at it.

I was assigned to teach in *Sektion Anglestik und Amerikanistik* (the Department of British and American Studies), which is housed in a building called *die Kommode* because it supposedly looks like a cabinet. The Kommode formerly served as the palace of the German Kaisers and is situated on Unter den Linden, a famous boulevard in the cultural center of East Berlin, and adjacent to Bebelplatz, the square where the Nazis burned thousands of banned books in 1933. The statue of Frederick the Great stands on Unter den Linden between the Kommode and the *Hauptgebaeude* (the main building of the university) in front of which stand statues of the Humboldt brothers, Wilhelm (the founder of Berlin University) and Alexander (a famous explorer in North America and the namesake of Humboldt State University in northern California).

I shared an office with about eight other colleagues in *Berich Amerikanistik* (subdepartment of American Studies). Our office included two desks with a telephone, a large couch and two small ones and a coffee table for Bereich meetings, and a large shelf of books. Due to the shortage of office space, my colleagues generally worked at home rather than in the Bereich office. In contrast, the Sektion head occupied a relatively large office which included a set of easy chairs for entertaining guests. Professor Horst Idhe, a specialist in African-American literature and the head of the subdepartment of American Studies, served as my *Betreuer* (caretaker) during the course of my stay at Humboldt University. In this capacity, we often met over lunch in the *Professora Mensa* (faculty dining room) and at various cafes to discuss not only my responsibilities at the university but also my observations of social life in the GDR.

At the opening session of the Department of British and American Studies in the Marx-Engels Hall of the Hauptgebaude, I was presented with a bouquet of yellow flowers to mark the beginning of my status as a visiting professor. In that capacity, my primary responsibility was to teach a course titled *Landeskunde der USA*. The German word *Landeskunde* does not have an English equivalent but essentially refers to the interdisciplinary study of a specific country. I lectured once a week to another group of fourth year language interpretation students and met every other week for two hours each with five different seminar groups of third year language students who were preparing to be teachers of either a German-English combination or a Russian-English combination. Each seminar group met with me on alternate weeks and with one of my colleagues on the other weeks. In some instances, my colleagues sat in on my lectures and seminars, but often they did not. Although my colleagues recommended that I cover certain topics, such as the American economy and the polity, they in no way attempted to influence the manner in which I taught.

Ironically, my reliance on a critical analysis of American society and textbooks such as Joe Feagin's *Social Problems* and Howard Zinn's *A People's History of the United States* prompted some of my students to ask me later on whether someone at the university had instructed me what to teach. On one occasion, my Betreuer told my colleagues in Bereich Amerikanistik (the subdepartment of American Studies) that I presented a "critical perspective" rather than a black-white one of American society, one which was good for their students to hear from an American. I am pleased to say that at no time was I instructed by the Council for International Exchange of Scholars (the organization that operates the Fulbright Program) to present a propagandistic portrayal of American society. Unfortunately, the booklets on American history, politics, and the American economy that the United States Information Agency (USIA) more than gladly provides Fulbright Lecturers with upon request in their teaching assignments abroad are so propagandistic that they would be an embarrassment to use in a serious examination of American society.

I was somewhat surprised at the reluctance of my students to either pose questions of me or to respond to my questions of them. Although a colleague gave the chairperson of the department a glowing report about my first lecture, I was disappointed that no one asked me a question either during or after it. My colleague complained that GDR students are not critical enough, but it appeared that years in the educational system taught most of them it was safer not to ask any questions than to ask the "wrong" one. Indeed, over time, a number of students admitted exactly this to me. Another factor that contributed to the students' shyness was their self-consciousness about their English-speaking abilities. Unlike many West German students who had many opportunities for improving their English-speaking abilities, East German students were generally not permitted to travel to the West and had exposure to very few English speakers within the borders of the GDR. A group of English language students once told me that their number one topic of conversation was not love (*Liebe*) but their inability to visit Great Britain or the United States in order to improve their English. Given these handicaps, I thought that the students in my department spoke English quite well, but it was difficult to convince them of this.

Unfortunately, many of the students in the department were not particularly motivated by the thought of becoming school teachers. Many of them had been rejected by the departments of their first choice and some hoped that they would be admitted into one of the more prestigious disciplines at some time in the future. I often found it difficult to find volunteers for the oral report that the department expected each one of them to do in class during the course of the semester. As a consequence, I often had to draft students for this assignment. In fact, on one occasion some of the more vocal students in one of my seminars recommended that I do this since apparently it was a practice that they had come to expect. In contrast to my students, I found the ethnography students who attended a talk that I gave on theoretical perspectives in American anthropology to be much more motivated. In part, they may have been more willing to pose questions because I had spoken in German. Furthermore, the fact that ethnography was their preferred field of study undoubtedly contributed highly to their interest in the content of lectures and seminars.

A practice that I found extremely irritating was a tendency on the part of the students to whisper in class. While in part this may have served as a way of alleviating the boredom of class, it apparently was a strategy for figuring out what the instructor was saying without asking him or her a direct question. They not only inflicted this behavior upon me but also upon their fellow students when the latter gave oral reports. On one such occasion, I complained that it was difficult for either me or students making the presentations to concentrate while a fair number of the students in the class were whispering. Despite my admonishment, some of them began to whisper to each other during my discussion of class material. I told the students that I was not sure whether their whispering in class was a general practice in the GDR, but that I would not tolerate it from them. After the seminar, a male student and a female student told me that the students asked one another questions because they were afraid to ask the instructor questions, in particular in the presence of a regular member of the faculty, lest their names be placed on a "black list" for posing the "wrong questions." The department chairperson said that he asks students to leave if they begin to whisper in his classes. He suggested that I shame the offending students by asking them a question and that I invite them to the *Cafe* to discuss the problem with them.

An American language instructor, who had taught in the department for several years, confessed to me that he had never managed to solve the whispering problem in his classes. He noted that one professor in the department once walked out of class because the whispering interfered so much with his lecture. My American colleague noted one faculty member attempted to outshout the students. He noted that whispering in particular was a problem in classes on Marxism-Leninist theory, which suggests that at least in part the pattern of whispering in class served as a subtle form of protest against the state. Students often complained about the dogmatic manner in which many instructors taught Marxism-Leninism. Conversely, I heard reports that some instructors taught Marxism-Leninism in a "revisionist" manner and were willing to deviate considerably from the party line. One of my colleagues who generally sat in when I taught in a section of Landeskunde der USA told me that my teaching style suggested that I enjoy teaching. He felt that I try to figure out where the students are coming from, prompting him to remark that at one time emphasis had been placed almost entirely on the collectivity in the GDR with the expectation that individuals conform to it. He maintained that in more recent years, however, the concept of *Individualitaet* (individuality) as opposed to *Individualismus* (individualism) had come to be accepted in the GDR.

On one occasion, I did have a minor breakthrough in motivating my students to speak English. On this particular day, the few males in the seminar group were absent and the women were generally shyer about speaking in classes, possibly for two reasons. Since most of the males in my seminar classes had spent 18 months in the military, the female students were generally younger and less worldly than the men. Furthermore, I suspect that they were conforming to some sort of pattern of GDR femininity by which women should not try to appear to be more intelligent than men. I teasingly asked my female students whether they found me so threatening that they were afraid to speak in class. I proposed that I speak in German so they could see that their English was better than my German. When I asked them questions in German, I only received responses when I called upon specific students to answer. At the end of the seminar, I invited the class to accompany me to a cafe where we could speak with one another in German as a strategy for them to lose some of their shyness. Most of the students had other commitments, but six accepted my invitation. As we walked along *Unter den Linden*, one of the students suggested that I speak in German and that they speak in English. The ice was broken. The students asked me all sorts of questions about American society and about my impressions of the GDR. They said that they didn't understand why the GDR state prohibited them from traveling to the West and asked me if they could visit the library in the U.S. embassy. I told them that I had heard that the GDR prohibited students from visiting the embassy, but that I would speak to the department chairperson to determine whether an exception could be made in their case. When I teased the students that since we had gotten better acquainted, I would now expect them to speak out more in class, one of them suggested that I just call upon them and another said that they were reluctant to speak out in class because they were "girls." I told them that since they were older than eighteen years, they would be defined as "women" in the United States. An American woman residing in West Berlin became so curious about our conversation in which I spoke in German and the students in English that she came over to our table to find out what was going on. When I told the department chairperson about the students' request to visit the U.S. embassy, he said that the GDR Supreme Court had ruled against GDR citizens visiting the embassy, except for special reasons, because the U.S. government accepted the FRG's policy of regarding all GDR citizens as FRG citizens and of granting passports to those who had defected to the FRG.

An amusing incident occurred when I visited a cafe with two students from another seminar class. Whereas the female student gave up her coat at the cloakroom (*Garderobe*), the male student and I hung our coats on the backs of our chairs. The waitress told the two of us that we would either have to give up our coats at the Garderobe or put them on in what was a rather overheated room. Finding her comment a bit amusing, or in retrospect a good example of Berliner sarcasm, I resorted to a little ethnomethodology (a research technique developed by sociologist Harold Garfinkel in which one learns the norms of a society by violating them) by asking her what would be wrong with leaving our coats on the back of our chairs. She replied that if we were permitted to do this, everyone in the cafe would want to do the same thing - an obvious violation of German

Ordnung (order). In the course of our conversation, my students told me that GDR citizens tried to cope with their sense of powerlessness by retreating into their private lives. The male student said that most university students were frustrated with and cynical about life in the GDR. The female student added that she knew of only one student who believed that the GDR was a wonderful country.

In addition to inviting students periodically to accompany me to cafes, another strategy that I used to become better acquainted with them was by sponsoring several parties. I suggested that if they purchased the refreshments for the parties, I would reimburse them, something which I could easily do since I had more than enough Ostmarks to take care of my own needs. The first of these parties took place in a student's apartment. Although most of the students felt shy about speaking English at first, several of them became more comfortable about doing so as the evening progressed. A male student expressed his alienation with life in the GDR by noting that one should just "be happy" - an expression that he borrowed from an American song popular at the time. The students said that they resented being required to take 30 to 32 hours of class room work a week and being allowed only a few electives in their program of study. They suspected that one of the members of their seminar group made reports about their actions and attitudes to the state, but were not sure who in their group functioned as an informer. The students complained about the privileges enjoyed by SED elites. One student told a GDR joke (*DDR Witz*) in which Erich Honecker tells a little girl that she may make one request of him. When she asks him to take down the Wall, he tells her that he cannot grant her wish because the two of them would be the only people left in the GDR. As I walked to the subway stop with two of the female students, one of them thanked me for making it possible for all of us to meet. As I returned to my apartment that night, I had the sense that I spent the evening with members of a "lost generation."

When I gave an end-of-semester party for one of my seminar groups at my apartment, one of the male students commented on what a great idea it was. The bored looks on the faces of the female students as he and I discussed the difficulties in creating a socialist society prompted me to suggest that we change the topic of conversation. I quietly told the students that they might want to be discreet in their comments since I had heard a rumor that my apartment might be bugged, but my warning did not deter them from expressing themselves. They complained that they had been forced to sign an agreement that they would not speak with any Westerners during the following semester when they were to study Russian at the Pushkin Institute in Moscow. The sole male student present complained that as teachers they will be expected to defend the GDR state, regardless of their personal opinions. The students complained that most of their teachers at the university treat them like little children. Although several students expressed a desire to visit the West, they expressed their commitment to their society, despite its flaws. The students gave me a stuffed dog as a goodbye present with the following note attached: "Hopefully, the barking of this nice, little dog will remind you dear Prof. Bear [sic] in a small and happy way of your months spent here in the GDR, our country, and the few lessons we had the opportunity to receive from you!"

Although many of my students appeared to be apolitical and expressed mixed feelings about the GDR as a manifestation of "actually existing socialism," on the whole they were considerably more progressive than the majority of American college students. This became apparent when I conducted mock U.S. presidential elections in several seminar classes. I obtained the idea for doing so from a mock election that had been held at an election night party at the U.S. Embassy in East Berlin on November 9, 1988. The embassy mock election tabulated the votes for the Americans and the Europeans present. The Americans consisted of embassy staff and visiting faculty and students in the GDR and the Europeans consisted of Western Europeans on the embassy staff and East German guests. Whereas Bush won by a landslide in the United States, as the table below indicates, he lost by a landslide in East Berlin on election night.

Table 1.
Mock Election at U.S. Embassy, East Berlin,
November 9, 1988.

	Bush	Dukakis	Write-In
Americans	10	29	6
Europeans	12	28	4

As the table below indicates, Bush lost mock elections in two of my five seminar classes even more decisively than at the embassy.

Table 2.
Mock Elections in Landeskunde der USA Seminars at Humboldt University, 1988.

	Bush	Dukakis	Write-In
Seminar Group 1	0	5	2
Seminar Group 2	0	10	0

The two write-in votes in group one were for Jesse Jackson and there was one abstention in group 2.

In addition to those at Humboldt University, I had some interesting experiences when I gave guest lectures at other GDR institutions of higher learning. On the occasion of my first visit to Rostock University, I spoke to a group of about 40 students and several faculty members about African-American religion (See Baer 1984 and Baer and Singer 1992) in the late afternoon, by which time it was quite dark in the northernmost major city in the GDR. In the last half hour of my lecture, all of the lights in the building, except for the small light at the lectern, went out due to a power failure. Afterwards, I remarked to my hosts that perhaps the spirits were trying to tell me something. Perhaps the most delightful experience in my entire teaching career occurred at the end of a lecture on religion in American society that I gave at the teachers' college in Potsdam. After my lecture two female students asked me to sign the notes that they had taken on it, something which made me feel a bit like a celebrity. When I told my hosts about this incident afterwards, one of them, an American who had been teaching for many years at the college, said that his students were more likely to throw their notes on his lectures away after class.

I received only one complaint about my actions as a visiting professor during my stay at Humboldt University. It did not concern my performance in the classroom but at a Free German Youth (FDJ or *Freie Deutsche Jugend*) party sponsored by my department. Along with other faculty members in the department, I was asked to give some sort of performance as part of the evening's festivities. Lacking any musical talents, I decided to tell a story about a personal experience in a faked Southern drawl to give the student a flavor for the type of English that is spoken in the region of the United States where I teach and two of the many GDR jokes that I had learned, one of which I told in English and the other which I told in German. While I suspect that most people in the audience couldn't understand my imitation of a Southern accent, the audience appeared to have responded well to my GDR jokes, at least for the most part. Afterwards, the department chairperson told me that he found the joke that I told about the GDR economy particularly humorous and another faculty member added that I seemed to have discovered how the GDR economy really functioned. About a week and a half later, one of my colleagues told me that a male student and a female student had told her that my jokes had been inappropriate in a public setting, particularly since I was a visiting professor. The following day, another colleague rebuked me for telling GDR jokes at the FDJ party. I apologized to him for having offended him and others by my actions and felt quite bad about having done so. However, when I told some of my students at a party that two students had complained about my behavior, they said that there was always someone in the GDR who would report one's action if one stepped out of line.

Conversely, faculty and students in universities did occasionally speak out against the policies of the GDR state. The most explicit instance of this in my experience occurred after the GDR state banned the publication of *Sputnik*, a Soviet version of *Readers' Digest*, in November 1988. Although the magazine had been considered merely another boring Soviet publication, its inclusion of more critical articles in the spirit of glasnost was not a development that overjoyed SED elites. A colleague told me that it was easier to obtain an English version of *Sputnik* than a German version in the GDR before the banning. The straw that broke the camel's back, so to speak, was an article that criticized the Hitler-Stalin pact. The banning of *Sputnik* provoked an outcry among faculty and students throughout the GDR, including within my department. A professor of Marxism-Leninism told me that none of the some three dozen colleagues with whom he discussed the affair approved of the banning. Many students and academic departments even wrote formal letters of protest to the GDR state, although the state chose to ignore their complaints - another indicator that SED elites were out of touch with the realities of social life in the GDR during its last days.

An Ami Footloose in East Berlin and the GDR

I had the opportunity during the six months or so that I resided in East Berlin as a Fulbright Lecturer to develop an extensive social network. Although I went to West Berlin several times during that time, including in order to visit some of my relatives, East Berlin became a second home for me. My stay there for about two months in early 1991 served to rejuvenate my attachment to the city. During my second stay in East Berlin, I also explored West Berlin much more thoroughly than I had done so while it was an isolated city-state situated within the GDR. Ironically, I developed a wider social network in East Berlin than I have ever developed in any of the many American cities where I have lived. In large part, this was true because I was determined to learn as much about life in East Berlin and the GDR as I could manage during a seven-month period.

My status as a Fulbright Lecturer allowed me to establish contact with many faculty and students at Humboldt University. Although I interacted with a fair number of my colleagues in the Department of British and American Studies at various places, only three of them, two of whom were visiting American instructors, invited me to visit them in their homes. The only East German colleague who invited me to visit her at her home was Helga Lumer, a specialist in Native American literature. She told me that members of the department don't socialize much with each other outside of the university setting. Helga is married to Bob Lumer, an American who met her on a visit from France. Bob decided to immigrate to the GDR so that he could live with Helga. He obtained a doctorate in history from Rostock University and worked for many years as a researcher in the Academy of Sciences. Helga and Bob introduced me to both the GDR Country Western and Indian club scenes which are described later in this chapter. Although a few other colleagues said that they would like to invite me to their homes, they never did so. I learned later that faculty members in the department rarely visited each other in their homes, a pattern perhaps not much different from one commonly found among American academics.

I also established a fair number of professional and personal relationships with faculty members in other departments at Humboldt University. I periodically got together with Guenther Rose, who taught Marxism-Leninism in the Department of Theology and had been a Fulbright Scholar in the United States during the 1987-1988 academic year. On 29 October 1988, he gave me a personal tour of Berlin. Professor Rose told me that the Wall was a contradiction - a violation of human freedom but yet a necessity given external factors. He felt that the process of eliminating the Wall was underway, in part reflected by the fact that many more GDR citizens were receiving permission to travel to the West than in the past. While he lamented that academics in the GDR lacked any good publishing outlets, Professor Rose said that he conducted open discussions about developments in the Soviet Union in his classes. Unfortunately, when I attempted to call Professor Rose in February 1991, his son told me that he had suffered a serious stroke during the Wende. Some people suggested that the changes in East Germany had contributed to his illness. I also periodically got together with Walter Rusch, an associate professor in the Department of Ethnography, and Professor Karl Sommer, the Director of the Institute of Anthropology at the School of Medicine, both of whom introduced me to the world of GDR anthropology as well as with Wilfred Wolf, an Assistant in the Department of Geography. Walter kindly permitted me to stay in his apartment in Prenzlauer Berg during my sabbatical in East Berlin in early 1991. I have visited him several more times since that time.

I also became acquainted with many East Berliners outside of academe, including civil servants, teachers, physicians, and workers. Ironically, most of my contacts with GDR workers developed through the Country Western scene in East Berlin. Despite the fact that I taught between 1976 and 1979 in Nashville, Tennessee, the home of Country Western music, and that Country Western music is quite strong in Arkansas, like most American academics, I have never had a strong interest in this aspect of white working-class culture. Much to my surprise, I learned through Helga and Bob that the GDR had a fairly robust Country Western subculture that in particular appealed to working-class East Germans. I attended my first Country Western dance at a restaurant in the Lichtenberg section of Berlin, which was attended by primarily young people but also by some middle-aged people. The dance was sponsored by the Range Riders, one of the several Country Western clubs in the GDR. The Berlin club had some 26 male and female members, but many others attended their parties. Roland Schrock, who served as the master of ceremonies for the evening's festivities, told me of plans to organize a Pony Express ride between Czechoslovakia and the GDR. He said that the clubs also hoped to eventually extend the ride to West Germany and France, but he did not have any clear-cut idea how this would be possible as long as the Wall was in place.

Several weeks later I visited the Plains Riders Saloon on the southern edge of East Berlin. In addition to dances at various eating locales, the Plains Riders of Berlin held about ten parties each year at their saloon, which looked fairly authentic. If I tuned out the German spoken by the East German workers dressed in cowboy, cowgirl, and bargirl clothing, I could easily imagine that I was back home in Arkansas. Roland told me that he was attracted to cowboy culture because of its *Freiheit* (freedom) and noted that the Country Western music expresses the sentiments of ordinary people such as himself. Petra Preussler, a school teacher, invited me to accompany her to one of the monthly Country Western dances, which were almost always sold out in advance, at the cultural center in Karlshorst, a suburb of Berlin. This event served as my best entree in GDR working-class culture because Petra introduced me to several of her working-class friends who worked at an East Berlin brewery who afterwards became important members of my social network.

In late November 1988, I gained some interesting insights when I went to eat lunch at the restaurant in my apartment complex on Karl Maron Strasse. I struck up a conversation with Juergen, a middle-aged man at my table who worked in a brewery that produced export beer for 660 Ostmarks a month. He told me that he supplemented his rather low wages by selling beer that he smuggled out of the brewery. Juergen said that he was divorced and wished to live a quiet life without lots of demands. He said that his father had been a Nazi, but he didn't feel personally responsible for the actions of his parents' generation. Prior to 1961 Juergen had worked as a receptionist and a waiter in a West Berlin hotel, but found many Westerners to be phonies. Conversely, he said that he detested the SED, particularly its members who joined the party for career reasons. Juergen claimed to have served Walter Ulbricht one time in coattails and white gloves and noted that SED elites lived very well. Juergen said that once when he was waiting on tables at a reception at the House of Soviet-German Friendship in East Berlin, a top-echelon Soviet bureaucrat gave him 500 Marks so he could quietly slip out of the building in order to avoid the world of protocol and secret service for a few hours. He asked me if I could *tausch* (exchange) eight Marks with him because he wanted to buy his daughter a Christmas calendar with windows that one opens as Christmas approaches in an *Intershop*, a chain of stores where GDR citizens could buy Western products with hard currency. I told him that I would exchange money with him at an equal rate rather than at the *Schwarzmarkt* (black market) rate since as a guest of the GDR state I did not want to break its laws. When I exchanged 20 Marks with him after we had finished our meal, Juergen exclaimed that our meeting had made it a very happy day for him.

During my stay in the GDR, I attended several political rallies in East Berlin as well as one in Frankfurt an Oder, which is situated on the Polish border. The one in Frankfurt an Oder occurred on 3 September 1988, and was sponsored by the Free German Youth, the Association of Journalists, and several other organizations in order to promote solidarity against imperialism. Posters calling for solidarity with the Nicaraguan and Salvadoran people, opposing the Pinochet dictatorship in Chile and apartheid in South Africa, demanding freedom for Nelson Mandela and the Sharpeville Six, support for UNICEF, were juxtaposed with American rock music, food stands, and a flea market.

On 11 September 1988, I attended the "International Commemoration for the Victims of Fascist Terrorism and the Struggle Against Fascist and Imperialist War" which started with tens of thousands of East Germans, including workers, FDJers in blue shirts and Young Pioneers in red kerchiefs, marching from Alexanderplatz to Bebelplatz where they listened to speeches by SED elites and by a visiting Soviet dignitary. On 7 October 1988, I witnessed the next to last *National Feiertag* (National Holiday) parade commemorating the formation of the GDR on that day in 1949. I was somewhat repulsed by the display of military hardware and personnel that proceeded down Karl Marx Alle from Strausberger Platz to Alexanderplatz given the emphasis on *Frieden* (peace) in the two earlier political rallies that I had attended. While many GDR citizens found the militaristic exhibition of this annual event distasteful, many in the crowd seemed to enjoy it.

I experienced almost complete freedom of movement during my stay in the GDR. On several occasions, however, members of the *Volkspolizei* (people's police) stopped me and requested my *Personalausweis* (personal identification card). With the exception of one instance, when this happened near East Berlin's *Hauptbahnhof* (main train station) around 10 p.m., these requests occurred after I walked a short distance from the U.S. Embassy. In each instance, apparently the policeman standing outside of the embassy walkie-talkied a colleague standing on a nearby street or outside of the train station on Freidrichstrasse, the main border crossing to West Berlin. I generally showed my American passport and explained that I was a visiting professor at Humboldt University. When I decided to show my Humboldt University faculty identification card as a sort of experiment, the police officer accepted it. In each instance, the police officer read my name and noted the fact that I am a U.S. citizen, apparently so that this information could be transmitted to a centralized information bank, thanked me, politely returned my identification, and terminated our interaction with a salute. The Volkspolizei in all probability, however, was more interested in identifying GDR citizens who had entered the embassy more than visiting American professors such as myself. At any rate, I learned to dodge the police stationed in the vicinity of the embassy by avoiding the side streets adjacent to it and walking along the grassy median strip on Unter den Linden in order to avoid the policeman stationed outside the British Embassy, a short distance from the American Embassy.

Perhaps influenced by old American films about life behind the Iron Curtain, I somehow had the impression before going to the GDR that I might be kept under constant surveillance. If this was the case, I certainly did not sense it in my extensive travels throughout the GDR. I cannot imagine that the state security agency followed me as I walked through the back streets and parks of East Berlin, Leipzig, Erfurt, Dresden, Rostock, Magdeburg, Potsdam, Stralsund, the hills and mountains of the southern GDR, and the beaches of the Baltic Sea or observed me in each and every one of the many restaurants, cafes, theaters, museums, and stores that I visited or watched me on the many train rides that I took. Undoubtedly they may have asked selected persons questions about me, but I certainly did not sense the omnipresent and watchful eye of "Big Brother" during my stay in the GDR.

While I did not visit by any means every nook and cranny of the GDR, I had the opportunity to see much of it, something not too difficult to accomplish in seven months time due to that country's compactness and the centrality of East Berlin. Within a few hours by train, I could reach Rostock, Schwerin, Stralsund, the island of Ruegen, or the Baltic Sea in the North or Dresden, Leipzig, Erfurt, Karl Marx Stadt (renamed Chemnitz after the unification) or various mountain ranges in the South. When I told a group of students once the places that I had visited in the GDR, they all agreed that I had seen more of their country than any of them had. I often had the feeling of being the exotic "other" in my travels around the GDR, particularly outside of East Berlin. I was often the first American with whom many of my East German contacts had ever interacted. When a friend took me to visit his favorite Gaststaette upon my arrival in Neubrandenburg, a medium-sized city in Mecklenberg, its *Chef* (manager) asked me to sign the guest book because I was the first American to have visited the establishment in his memory.

Travel on the Deutsche Reichsbahn (DR), the GDR's rail system, was considerably more primitive than travel on the Deutsche Bundesbahn (DB), the FRG's rail system. East German trains were considerably slower than West German trains and much more likely to be late. Furthermore, they were generally packed on Friday and Sunday evenings, even more so than in West Germany, as throngs of students and soldiers made weekend trips to and from home in order to visit parents and friends. As a result, many passengers had to stand wherever they could find room. Furthermore, windows and restrooms almost always were dirty. During cold weather, train cars often were either overheated or cold. Despite these inconveniences, I found travel by train in the GDR to be both a bit of a challenge and an adventure that provided opportunities to speak with ordinary GDR citizens about a wide variety of topics.

Unfortunately, finding a hotel room in the GDR proved to be very difficult, particularly since I wanted to stay at GDR hotels instead of Interhotels where Westerners had to pay in hard currency. Making hotel reservations well in advance didn't suit my spur-of-the-moment style of traveling, although the Office of International Relations at Humboldt University was willing to make the necessary arrangements. The office arranged for my overnight stay in a guest room at the Technical University in Dresden on one occasion and my hosts arranged for me to stay in a guest room upon my two visits to Wilhelm Pieck University in Rostock. I actually only stayed in a GDR hotel on one occasion, that of an overnight stay in Leipzig. On that occasion, the hotel clerk initially quoted me a price of 68 Ostmarks - the rate apparently for Westerners - for a simple but clean room. When I showed my Humboldt University identification card and a letter from the Ministry of Higher Education stating that I could stay in GDR hotels for GDR prices, the receptionist charged me 24 Marks for my room.

I discovered the difficulty of finding a room in a GDR hotel on a beautiful weekend in September of 1988 when I took the train to Bad Schandau, a resort town on the Elbe in the *Saechsische Schweiz* (Saxon Switzerland). Unfortunately, the town's sole hotel was booked up. After wandering around Bad Schandau, I took one of the many boats that ply up and down the Elbe (the East German version of the Rhine) to Koeningstein which, much to my surprise, had no hotels in operation. After looking around the town, I took a train to Kurort Rathan where I learned that the village's two hotels also were completely booked. Again after looking around, I took a train to Dresden where I also was unable to find a hotel room, at least not for Ostmarks. Without a place to stay for the night, I had little other choice than to return to East Berlin. Nevertheless, the scenic mountains, rock formations, and picturesque villages, despite their shabbiness, had made what turned out to be a long Saturday outing worthwhile.

The train ride from East Berlin to Dresden on that Saturday provided me with my first encounter with East German "hooligans." The train was jam packed with young male *Fussball* (football or soccer) fans on their way to watch a match between the Berlin team and the Dresden Dynamos.

Most of them stood outside of the passenger compartments where they drank beer, carried on, and verbally harassed passengers who tried to squeeze their way along the train's corridors. Many of these young working-class men wore their hair very shortly cropped, not quite short enough to qualify them as "skinheads" which the GDR state had suppressed several years earlier. An argument developed between a conductor and several soccer fans while I was eating in the *Mitropa* (dining car). When he asked for their tickets, they claimed that they had left them in their compartment. This confrontation was followed by an argument with the waiter as to how much they had eaten. The young men spoke in a quite abusive manner with the waiter, and one of them sarcastically addressed him in the familiar *du* rather than in the formal *Sie*. Two or three train policemen (*Schutzpolizei*) patiently observed the entire scene but did not interfere. When the train arrived in Dresden, the some two or three hundred soccer fans chanted soccer cheers and phrases such as "Hooligans, hooligans!" and "Sieg Heil!" as they marched down the platform. As the mob descended the stairs and turned right to exit the train station, several policemen, one of whom held a muzzled German shepherd that was barking madly, stood guard and followed them, apparently on their way to the soccer stadium. The proceedings that I had observed on the train that morning seriously challenged the belief that the GDR constituted a "totalitarian" society.

I made what may have been my most unique excursion in the GDR when I accompanied my colleague Helga Lumer to a meeting of representatives of the GDR's Indian clubs in a village outside of Leipzig. Before the meeting, we visited the clubhouse and the tepees of the Mandan group which drew its members from the Leipzig area. Representatives of the Mandan Club said that their group consisted of 22 individuals belonging to six families who spent much of their free time during the warm weather months by recreating as much as possible the traditional lifestyle of Native Americans. The Indian clubs were affiliated with the GDR state's *Kulturbund* (cultural league), but appeared to have had a considerable degree of autonomy. Most of the adult members of the clubs were in their twenties and thirties with counter cultural tendencies (e.g., many of the men wore long hair). One representative told me that the Indian clubs function like familial groupings. While the clubs did not have an explicitly political orientation, many members were concerned about the GDR's ecological crisis. Some members subscribed to a romanticized image of Native American cultures, but others made efforts to work in solidarity with Native Americans political movements - a pattern which converged with the GDR state's critique of the racist and imperialist policies of advanced capitalist countries, particularly the United States. One representative lamented, however, that it was safer to criticize environmental problems on the Navajo reservation than in the GDR. The Indian clubs, which continue to exist in East Germany, constituted one of the many spaces that East Germans created for themselves within the authoritarian strictures of the GDR state. Undoubtedly, the Ministry for State Security (*Ministerium fuer Stattssicherheit* or *Stasi*) had infiltrated these groups but regarded them as a relatively harmless safety valve. I was reminded once more how small the world is when I again met a few of the representatives of the Indian clubs when they visited friends in Conway, Arkansas, in August 1991.

Cabarets served as another safety valve in the GDR. On 27 September 1988, I attended a performance of *Wir Handeln Uns Was Ein* at *Die Distal* on Freiderichstrasse in East Berlin. A colleague was delighted to accompany me because tickets to *Die Distel* were difficult to obtain. My connection for obtaining two tickets was an acquaintance in the United States Embassy. I was rather surprised at the extent to which various aspects of GDR society, including the state plan, inefficiency in the work place, Erich Honecker, travel restrictions, the private sector of the economy, and restrictions on dissent and glasnost, were lampooned in the skits performed. In one skit, an East Berlin woman, who sat in a stand selling *Obst* (fruit), and a West Berlin woman, who sat in a stand selling *Suedfrucht* (Southern fruit), compared their respective wares. They were separated by a line of brief cases obviously symbolizing the Wall. Another skit portrayed the confusion that a West German corporate manager experienced when he was given the opportunity to supervise work in a GDR state firm. In yet another skit, an East German attempted to stay in an Interhotel which he had helped to construct by telling the receptionist that he was from Philadelphia. The receptionist gave him the royal treatment until she discovered that he could pay for his stay only with Ostmarks. While my colleague found the performance as amusing as I did, a friend told me that she did not enjoy visiting *Die Distel* because she could not laugh at the things that were lampooned there.

Although I did not spend much time investigating religious life in the GDR, because of my previous research on Mormonism (Baer 1988), I decided to visit the site of the Mormon temple in Freiberg, a small city on the edge of the Erzegebirge in Saxony in February 1989. The Freiberg Temple was the only Mormon temple in a post-revolutionary society. Unfortunately, since I am a "Gentile" (a Mormon term for a non-Mormon), I was not able to visit the interior of the temple. In the Visitors' Center, Herr Georg Birsefelder, a Swiss retiree, provided me with an account of the status of Mormons in the GDR. He and his wife, Anna, were serving as the first Mormon missionaries in the GDR, but were permitted by the GDR state only to give information about the Mormon Church at the Visitors' Center. In October 1988 Erich Honecker, the General Secretary of the SED, and other GDR leaders in a meeting with Mormon leaders Gordon B. Hinckley and Thomas Monson agreed to permit Mormon missionaries to proselytize in the county beginning in April 1989.

Herr Birsefelder reported that there were some 4,000 Mormons in the GDR. Prior to World War II, the area that became the GDR had about 12,000 Mormons, most of whom later emigrated to the FRG or the United States. The first Mormon ward (congregation) in East Germany was established in Dresden in 1855. Herr Birsefelder said that the Mormon Church (officially called the Church of Jesus Christ of Latter-day Saints) exhibited a relatively slow pattern of growth in the GDR, particularly in comparison to certain other European countries, such as Portugal. Henrik Burkhardt, a physician, served as the President of the Mormon Church in the GDR and the President of the Freiberg Temple. The president of the Freiberg stake (a district consisting of wards or branches) was the proprietor of a small auto electronics shop. Three types of Mormon congregations existed in the GDR: (1) the *Gemeinde* or ward, (2) the *Zweig* or branch, and 3) the *Gruppe* or group consisting of a small number of members. The Freiberg stake consisted of 20 congregations (4 wards, 11 branches, and 5 groups) (*Kirche Jesu Christi der Heiligen der Letzen Tage, DDR*, n.d.).

Herr Birsefelder said he did not perceive any overt antagonism between Mormons and other religious groups in Freiberg. He added that the Mormon Church did not maintain formal ties with other religious bodies in the GDR. A state combine based in Karl Marx Stadt began to construct the Freiberg Temple in April 1983. Prior to the dedication of the Freiberg Temple in 1985, many GDR Mormons faced difficulty in visiting Mormon temples in other parts of Europe, including the one in Frankfurt am Main in the FRG. Some combined visits to relatives in the FRG with visits to temples in Western European countries (The Frankfurt Temple was not dedicated until 1987). In addition to GDR Mormons, the Freiberg Temple was intended to serve Mormons in other Eastern European countries. Hungary granted official recognition to the Mormon Church in 1988 and a LDS ward house was opened in Warsaw, Poland, several years ago.

In contrast to the situation in the United States where the Mormon Church plays a significant role in the politics of Utah and other states in the Intermountain West, in the GDR it eschewed overt political involvements. While some Mormons apparently belonged to the Christian Democratic Union, Biesefelder did not think it would be appropriate for a Mormon to belong to the Socialist Unity Party because of its atheistic philosophy. He read several quotes from the writings of Lenin that guarantee religious freedom under socialism. Mormons could support the GDR's family policies and health care system and serve in the GDR military. Herr Birsefelder felt that Mormon children didn't experience overt discrimination. While he said that membership in FDJ was a matter for parental discretion, he had never seen a Mormon child in a FDJ uniform.

The brief chapter of Mormonism in the former GDR raises some interesting sociological questions. Why, given that in many ways Mormonism has incorporated American value orientations and essentially functions as a theocratic multinational corporation within the capitalist world system, did the GDR leaders permit a rapprochement between the GDR state and the Mormon church? Despite their obvious differences, the two had arrived at some significant convergences. Like the Mormon church, the GDR state emphasized a strong family policy and work ethic, which it viewed as essential to the construction of a developed socialist society.

Rainier Hagan, a scholar at the GDR's Institute of International Relations in East Berlin, told me that the Mormon Church's emphasis on education and "clean living" had made a favorable impression on GDR leaders. Although the GDR state had achieved a rapprochement of sorts with the Evangelical church, it was a tenuous one because the latter provided a sanctuary for the alternative peace, environmental, and human movements and for individuals who wanted to leave the GDR. In contrast, the Mormon Church discouraged its members from becoming involved in political protest and encouraged them to become model GDR citizens to the extent that their religious principles permitted. The Erzebirge area where the Freiberg Temple is situated in one where some of my more distant East German relatives reside. Unfortunately, I did not have the opportunity to visit them. However, I became acquainted with my most immediate East German relatives during my stay in the GDR, namely those who live in Magdeburg. I unsuccessfully attempted to visit a distant cousin during a stopover in Karl Marx Stadt. Since, like the vast majority of GDR citizens, he did not have a telephone, I took a streetcar to his apartment in a Neubau area of the city. His neighbor told me that I had missed him by about a half an hour. Unfortunately, I could not wait for him to return because I had to catch the last train to East Berlin. This incident illustrates the frustrations of trying to connect with people who did not have a private telephone. I stayed with my cousin Georg Nachtwei and his wife, Ruth, on three occasions during my stay in the GDR, in late October 1988, in mid-December 1988, and in late January 1989. They in turn took me to visit some of my other relatives, including my aunt, in Magdeburg. Georg is the son of one of my mother's brothers, who also was called Georg.

While Georg and Ruth were not necessarily typical GDR citizens, they by no means were atypical GDR citizens. Their lives certainly in many ways fit in a modal pattern that was more or less shared by many GDR citizens. My deceased uncle, Georg, joined the Social Democratic Party (SPD) after World War II and became a member of the Socialist Unity Party (SED) when the SPD and the Communist Party (KPD) merged in 1946 in the Soviet Sector of Germany. My uncle, however, left the SED when his small machine shop was collectivized. Unlike his father, my cousin never joined the SED, but this did not prevent him from obtaining an degree in civil engineering from the *Fachhochschule* (technical college) in Erfurt. Georg and Ruths' sole child, my nephew Georg, also never joined the SED but nevertheless managed to earn two doctorates, a PhD and a DSc in physics, from Humboldt University. He conducted research in solid state physics at Humboldt University, but was on leave at Oxford University during my stay in the GDR. Fortunately, I did have an opportunity to visit with Georg, Jr., and his family in East Berlin during early 1991. Subsequently, he took a position at Muenster University in West Germany.

My cousin worked for a heating equipment production firm in Magdeburg where he earned a monthly salary of 1,500 Ostmarks. Ruth worked as an accountant in Magdeburg's Centrum, the state department store. Georg and Ruth lived in a compact *Altbau* (old construction) apartment consisting of a living room, bedroom, kitchen, and bathroom in the Neustadt section of Magdeburg – a neighborhood where three generations of Nachtweis have lived. During the warm weather months Georg and Ruth spent much of their free time at their small *Gartenhaus* or *Dachua* outside of Magdeburg to which they drove in their Trabant, the two cylinder automobile which received so much attention in the West at the time of the Wende. The Trabant that they had at the time of my visits was their fourth. Georg said that used Trabants could be obtained on the Schwarzmarkt for a higher price than that for a new Trabant. Georg told me that although he was not pro-capitalist, he resented the manner in which the GDR state treated its citizens. He complained that the state provided them with a good education, but denied them freedom of expression. Georg, who takes great pride in his work, lamented that workplaces in the GDR were characterized by low morale, poor motivation, and petty jealousies. Georg and Ruth complained that the GDR placed pressure on workers to attend political rallies and assemblies and receptions for SED elites by granting bonuses only to those who regularly did so. Georg described the search for many household furnishings, such as the large cabinet in their living room, as a *Jagd* (hunt). He felt that many GDR citizens developed a type of pent-up aggression due to the frustrations associated with difficulties of obtaining certain consumer items. Conversely, he felt that the level of consumption in the GDR was just high enough to keep the general populace relatively docile, unlike the situation during the 1980s in Poland.

Chapter 2

The Legitimation Crisis in the German Democratic Republic Before the Wende: Views from Below

In this chapter, I argue that a "legitimation crisis" - a term that Habermas (1975) applied to late capitalism - existed in the German Democratic Republic prior to the Wende of 1989. In supporting this thesis, I draw upon the views held by GDR citizens with whom I spoke during 1988-1989 toward SED elites and functionaries, the economy, and the media. Despite the existence of a legitimation crisis in the GDR, I found that most of my subjects were committed to the social construction of socialism in their society. Whereas the term "socialism" had apparently become a dirty word in many other Eastern European societies, my observations indicated that many East Germans continued to subscribe to it as an ideal, even if they recognized that GDR society fell short of it. Peter and Fran Marcuse made a similar observation at the beginning of their stay in the GDR during 1989-1990. He notes: "Our initial experience, after our arrival in mid-August (three months before the opening of the Berlin Wall), suggested a schizophrenic society: no one we spoke to defended the political structure, yet almost everyone professed a continued commitment to socialism and took the prevailing political and social structure for granted, expecting, at best, small incremental changes here and there" (Marcuse 1991:9).

While the extent to which the views of my subjects were shared by the GDR populace is difficult to determine, various polls conducted before the election of March 1990 which presented the conservative Alliance for Germany headed by the Christian Democratic Union with the largest bloc of votes also suggest that a majority of GDR citizens favored the development of some form of democratic socialism in their society, at least up until that event. In the wake of Wende, Aronowitz observed,

A recent survey of 600 randomly chosen East Berliners found that 55 percent were still for a more equitable, democratically controlled socialism, and 30 percent favored free market socialism. It appears that the major demand in this more economically developed country focuses on political democratization, and the end of Communist Party rule rather than a return to capitalism (Aronowitz 1990:5).

Views of the GDR State from Below

I received the impression before I went to the GDR that its citizens would be reluctant to speak openly to me as an American, even as a progressive one, about the contradictions of their society. While certainly various individuals were guarded, at least initially, in our discussions, I was surprised how frank and candid many GDR subjects were. Some noted that they had come to feel much freer in expressing their opinions in the past decade or so, at least in certain settings, than they did in the past. For many GDR citizens, particularly those employed outside of the university and various government agencies involved in international relations, I was the only American with whom they had ever had an extended conversation. Many GDR citizens noted that the recent sociopolitical changes in the Soviet Union had contributed to a growing willingness to speak more openly in public places, including classrooms, restaurants, cafes, taverns, and public transportation carriers, about their society.

The SED Elite and State Functionaries

Unlike the one-party system in the Soviet Union, the GDR prior to the opening of the Wall had five political parties. The SED, which resulted from a merger in 1946 of the Communist Party and the Social Democratic Party, had been a Marxist-Leninist ruling party since the creation of the GDR state in 1949. The Democratic Farmers' Party consisted primarily of "working farmers;" the Christian Democratic Union was "committed to peace, human dignity and social justice" and the construction of socialism; the Liberal Democratic Party consisted of "craftsmen, retailers and intellectuals;" and the National Democratic Party consisted of "members of the former middle classes" (Panorama DDR 1986). Several of my subjects argued that party pluralism was more a matter of form than substance in the GDR since the non-ruling parties acquiesced to the SED leadership on most matters and, therefore, had no clear-cut identity within the GDR state. Most citizens found admission to the SED relatively easy in that it required nomination by two party members and a pro-forma allegiance to the state. In mid-1984, 2,238,283 people, or 17 percent of the population over age 18, belonged to the SED (Krisch 1985). While many GDR citizens viewed SED membership as an absolutely necessary criterion for career advancement, many others chose not to join the party because they didn't want to pay monthly dues or felt that they had to support objectionable policies. Rank-and-file SED members often argued, however, that relatively open discussions occurred at the lower echelons of the party but became increasingly difficult at higher levels.

Many GDR citizens, including rank-and-file SED members, maintained that SED elites, particularly members of the Politburo, enjoyed amenities that flagrantly violated socialist principles. SED elites were often criticized for living in spacious houses and guarded compounds, such as the one in Wandlitz - a village about 30 kilometers north of Berlin. Party elites were often criticized for being chauffeured around in shining black Volvos rather than in Wartburgs, the more expensive of the two GDR produced automobiles. Some GDR citizens referred to Wandlitz as "Volvograd." GDR citizens often spoke of specialty shops where party elites purchased Western products or high-quality GDR products for relatively low prices, whereas the GDR populace had to purchase the former in Intershops with hard (Western) currency or in high-priced *Delikat* food stores or *Equisit* clothing shops with GDR currency. Some of my subjects justified, although ambivalently, the amenities enjoyed by party elites on the grounds that they had to present an affluent image when meeting with foreign diplomats and business people from capitalist countries. Several subjects, including SED members, felt the party elite had evolved into a "new class" or doubted whether its members were true socialists. Conversely, others criticized middle-level state functionaries who shielded the elites from the social realities of GDR life. Before a party dignitary visited a state facility, state functionaries often reportedly ordered a window-dressing of the facility's interior and surroundings. Middle-level state functionaries rewarded workers with a bonus for regular appearances at receptions for party elites or at political rallies and parades. An economist, who joined the SED as a youth and argued that he couldn't quit the party without jeopardizing his position, objected vehemently to the "petit bourgeois" life-style and "Stalinist" perspectives of certain middle-level state functionaries.

Most GDR citizens feared the Ministry for State Security (*Ministerium fuer Stattssicherheit*), commonly referred to as the *Stasi*. According to Krisch (1985), the Stasi employed some 17,000 full-time staff members, of whom about 8,000 were uniformed officers, and purportedly an additional 100,000 informers. Many GDR citizens, however, believed that up to one out of every ten GDR adults worked for or collaborated with the Stasi in its surveillance activities. GDR citizens often speculated as to which individuals in their residential areas were Stasi employees or collaborators, and many university staff members and students maintained that each seminar group had at least one Stasi collaborator who reported upon remarks made by faculty and students. Some GDR citizens viewed the Stasi as a "state within a state" with a life of its own, which included political corruption as source of material enrichment for Stasi officials. Conversely, some subjects questioned whether the pervasiveness of the Stasi was as great as popular belief maintained, but admitted that the Stasi carefully monitored potential pockets of dissent, particularly among peace and environmental groups which had found a sanctuary within the Protestant churches.

The Economy

Despite damage to the infrastructure as the result of World War II, the war reparations in terms of infrastructure and labor power exacted by the Soviet Union following World War II, the lack of critical mineral and energy resources (such as iron ore, petroleum, and natural gas), and the lack of Marshall Plan financial assistance, the economic expansion that the GDR achieved, particularly during the 1960s and 1970s, had provided GDR citizens with the highest material standard of living in Eastern Europe. In describing the GDR economy during the early 1980s, Krisch observed:

> On a world scale, the GDR's per capita GNP ranks it behind most Western countries but still among the twenty highest and ahead of or on par with such countries as Italy, New Zealand, or Great Britain. In labor productivity its rank is even with

that of Great Britain but some 30 percent below France or West Germany (Krisch 1985:30).

The GDR state projected that its housing construction program would have provided modest but adequate housing for every GDR family and citizen sometime in the early 1990s. In addition to new housing developments, many older dwelling units had been restored or renovated in the GDR. Rent for housing was very inexpensive in comparison to advanced capitalist countries, ranging from 50 Marks per month with utilities being paid separately for a three- or four-room apartment in an older residential area to 200 Marks per month including utilities for a comparably sized apartment within easy reach of Alexanderplatz in the center of East Berlin. While GDR citizens often complained about the drabness of the Neubau (new construction) areas or the deterioration in many older apartments, most GDR citizens credited the state for its achievements in housing construction. On weekends or in the summer, a substantial minority of the GDR populace, including factory workers, retreated to garden houses of varying size. A faculty member at Greifswald University said that some 30 of his 50 departmental colleagues own garden houses.

GDR citizens could purchase relatively inexpensive *Lebensmittel* (foodstuffs), such as meat, dairy products, bread, cake, potatoes, red cabbage, and apples. Other vegetables, such as lettuce and tomatoes, and most fruits, particularly bananas, generally were available in limited amounts and in season. A growing number of health-conscious GDR citizens complained about the high carbohydrate, sugar and fat content of the standard GDR diet and the low availability of more nutritious foodstuffs. Also many subjects maintained that many higher quality meat and dairy products that could once be purchased in the *Kaufhalle* (grocery store) had to be purchased for much higher prices in the Delikat shops. Housing, public transportation (20 *Pfenning* for a street car, subway, bus, or one-zone rapid transit train ride in East Berlin), remained inexpensive; however, electronics equipment, clothing, household furnishings, and automobiles were expensive. Many complained that they generally had to order a new automobile about 12 or 13 years before delivery. The two-cylinder Trabant cost about 12,000 to 13,000 Marks and the Wartburg, which included a Volkswagon engine, cost over 30,000 Marks. Furthermore, spare automobile parts were generally difficult to obtain. GDR citizens often complained that the state exported many of the best GDR products to capitalist countries for hard currency. Also many GDR citizens complained about the difficulty of obtaining a room in a standard hotel or a table in a restaurant while many rooms and restaurants in Interhotels designated for Western guests paying hard currency were empty, particularly during the off season.

Several subjects argued that the state plan, supply shortages, cautious managerial policies, and a 8 3/4 hour work day produced low worker motivation, inefficiency, and morale. Some also asserted that many high-paying positions, some of which were held by retired military personnel, were economically superfluous, and that many GDR workers stole supplies and materials from their firms for personal use or for sale in the shadow economy. Furthermore, the GDR state had increasingly come to import sophisticated technology from advanced capitalist countries, a practice which further exacerbated the drive for hard currency and the economic dependency of the GDR on the capitalist world-system. Despite serious contradictions in the economy, the GDR had evolved into a consumer society with a relatively high material standard of living which was the envy of people in the Soviet Union, Poland, and other Eastern European societies. An increasing number of GDR citizens were beginning to question the environmental consequences of their culture of consumption. I often heard GDR citizens complain about the severe industrial pollution in cities such as Halle, Bitterfeld, Karl Marx Stadt, and Leipzig and the impact of acid rain on the *Erzgebirge* (Ore Mountains), a range in the southwestern GDR. East Berliners often joked that the Wall prevented smog from passing over from West Berlin and that their own city, unlike West Berlin, had no need for smog alerts. Many GDR citizens resented the state's willingness to provide land as a repository for Western waste products in exchange for hard currency.

The Media

In contrast to other East European countries, most GDR citizens found themselves in a unique situation in that most of them resided within easy access of FRG television and radio reception. In addition to DDR1 and DDR2, GDR citizens could watch three FRG television channels, including SAT 1, which specialized in the transmission of American films and serials. Furthermore, those East Berliners who understood English could listen to broadcasts from the American and British armed forces networks in West Berlin. The GDR state had come to accept that its populace relied heavily upon the Western media, both for news and entertainment, and planned to install a cable relay that would have transmitted FRG television channels to the Dresden area, which because of its terrain was unable to receive ordinary transmission from the FRG.

Many GDR citizens found information disseminated on GDR television and radio, in *Neues Deutschland* (the SED daily newspaper), in local newspapers, and in GDR state-operated popular magazines simplistic, propagandistic, and boring. They complained about news coverage that stressed the achievement of productivist goals and the reception of foreign dignitaries by SED elites. Intellectuals also lamented that the state permitted limited opportunities to publish critical analyses of GDR society. Some of my subjects maintained that news coverage, however, tended to portray social reality more accurately in local newspapers, particularly the *Berliner Zeitung*, than did *Neues Deutschland*, which one university faculty member described as a showcase on GDR life for the outside world. Some local newspapers, for example, occasionally presented cautious reports on environmental pollution in the GDR.

In its last years, the GDR state had made it increasingly difficult or impossible for GDR citizens to read certain Soviet publications and to view certain Soviet films. Only the Russian edition of *Pravda* was sold in the GDR, whereas the German edition was available in other German-speaking countries. The GDR state confiscated the first three 1988 issues of the Soviet weekly magazine *Neue Zeit* for "technical reasons." According to one SED member, whereas GDR intellectuals once regarded *Neue Zeit* to be a boring propaganda tabloid, they came to regard it as the most interesting and provocative current affairs periodical available in the GDR. The GDR state did not distribute Gorbachev's book, *Perestroika*, and distributed Soviet-published booklets on recent policy developments in the Soviet Union on a very limited basis. In November 1988 the GDR state banned further distribution of *Sputnik*, a Soviet monthly magazine, as well as five Soviet films, several of which were being shown at the time in the GDR. The GDR state cited an article in the November issue of *Sputnik* that posed the question, "Would Hitler have been possible without Stalin?" as the rationale for banning the increasingly popular Soviet periodical, which generally was available only in limited supply. The banning of *Sputnik* prompted an undercurrent of opposition in GDR society, including among SED members. Some university students wrote letters of protest to university administrators and state agencies about the banning. One university professor told me that in discussions with some three dozen colleagues about the *Sputnik* banning, he did not find one voice supporting the state's actions.

The state's imposed restrictions on information dissemination prompted many GDR citizens to rely on the FRG and other Western broadcasts for much of their news, not only on current events in the West but also in the GDR, the Soviet Union, and other Eastern European countries. FRG broadcasts served as the principal vehicle by which GDR citizens learned about sociopolitical developments in the Soviet Union. Evangelical church periodicals occasionally reported on controversial aspects of GDR society, such as environmental pollution. When the state censored an article in a church newspaper, the editorial staff of this newspaper decided to publish their next issue with a blank space where the banned article was slated to appear as a form of silent protest. While the other GDR political parties published newspapers of their own, GDR citizens generally did not consider them as viable alternative media outlets.

Conceptions of Socialism in the GDR and Responses to Glasnost and Perestroika

Marx and Engels refrained from drawing up a detailed blueprint of what form or forms socialism and communism would take. Nevertheless, a perusal of their writings indicates that they believed that socialism would exhibit four basic components: (1) public ownership of the means of production, (2) increasing social equality, (3) proletarian democracy, and (4) developed productive forces. The historical reality that successful socialist-inspired revolutions have occurred in the periphery rather than in core capitalist nations, as classical Marxists believed would be the case, has contributed to a considerable amount of debate among Western Marxist scholars and even some Eastern European Marxist scholars on the nature of post-revolutionary societies. Characterization of societies, such as the Soviet Union and other Eastern European states, China, Vietnam, Cuba, and Mozambique, tend to fall into one of the falling categories: (1) state or actually-existing socialism, (2) transitional forms between capitalism and socialism, (3) state capitalism, and (4) new class societies or social formations (see Clawson, et al. 1981; Markus 1982; Chase-Dunn 1982).

The GDR state defined itself as a "developed socialist state" with a democratic constitution, elected assemblies, and authoritative bodies gathered around the leadership of the working class and its party, the SED (Panorama DDR 1986). Certain GDR Marxist intellectuals called into question this definition of the GDR state. Robert Havemann (1972), an SED member and an eminent Humboldt University physical chemist, began to argue in the early 1960s that authentic socialism combined economic planning and political democracy and argued that remnants of Stalinist dictatorship prevented the development of democratic and ecologically sensitive socialism in the GDR. Havemann lost his professorship, was expelled from the SED, and was even placed under house arrest for two-and-a-half years for his critical writings and public statements on the GDR state.

Rudolf Bahro (1978), another SED member and former youth league official and economic administrator, argued in a book originally published in the FRG that "actually existing socialism" in the Soviet Union and other Eastern European societies, including the GDR, constituted a non-capitalist road to industrialization. He argued that actually existing socialism resembles the Asiatic mode of production in that its form of domination is based on state control rather than on private property. Bahro called for a democratized party, termed the "League of Communists," and rational economic planning that would be sensitive to both social needs and the natural environment. In August 1977 the GDR state arrested Bahro, but allowed him to emigrate to the FRG in October 1979 following an international campaign for his release.

While only a few GDR citizens had read Havemann's and Bahro's books, many members, particularly the intelligentsia, appear to have had some familiarity with them. Regardless of whether or not GDR citizens had read or even heard about the views of Havemann and Bahro on the GDR state, they formed a variety of interpretations on the nature of their society. Many, if not most, GDR citizens regarded the GDR as a socialist society because the means of production had been nationalized, but also regarded it as an imperfect form of socialism which needed to undergo a process of democratization. Many rank-and-file SED members admitted that the GDR as a socialist society manifested many contradictions related to external and internal factors that shaped its historical development. One professor of Marxism-Leninism told me that the development of socialism would involve several drawn-out stages, just as did the development of capitalism.

Other subjects noted that the unequal currency exchange imposed by FRG and West Berlin banks prior to the erection of the Wall permitted many FRG citizens and West Berliners to consume GDR products at very low prices, and thus posed a serious threat to the GDR economy. Many GDR citizens told me that they desired the opportunity to travel to the West before retirement age, at which time the GDR state permitted unrestricted travel to the West, but would also return to the GDR for personal reasons and because they were committed to the construction of a socialist society. These people resented that the GDR state did not trust them.

Many subjects complained that their state treated them like children and were very suspicious of many of the official statements made by SED elites and state functionaries. GDR youth in particular appeared to resent the paternalistic treatment accorded them by SED elders and expressed their dissatisfaction in a vary of ways, including consumerism, emulation of Western lifestyles, and involvement in peace and environmental groups. Some young GDR people became "punks" and, prior to state prohibition, a few experimented with the neo-fascist "skin-head" lifestyle. A fair number of young GDR males identified themselves as "hooligans" and followed their favorite soccer teams around the GDR on week-ends, while others wore Soviet military jackets or T-shirts inscribed with phrases such as "U.S. Marines," "Beverly Hills Police Department," or "United States Department of Defense." My conversations with university students often left me with the sense that I was interacting with members of a "lost generation" whose sole goal in life, as an American lyric popular in the GDR at the time suggested, was to be to "be happy."

Most GDR citizens believed that serious discrepancies existed in the GDR between the ideals and the realities of socialism. While they generally recognized that advanced capitalist societies, including the FRG, exhibit deep contradictions, such as poverty and high levels of unemployment, they often felt that their state did not provide them with an accurate portrayal of life in the West. Conversely, many of my subjects believed that advanced capitalist societies tended to be more democratic, provided greater freedom of expression, were economically more efficient, and provided greater access to material comforts. I often had the impression that many GDR citizens held an idealized view of life in the West - one that was conditioned by their viewing of Western films and television programs and the credibility gap they perceived in terms of what the GDR state told them about life in the West. When I pointed out that the relatively high material standard of living for the majority in the advanced capitalist countries, such as the FRG and the United States, is in part related to the impoverishment and underdevelopment of the Third World, many GDR citizens agreed with me in theory, but had difficulty recognizing this in reality. Most of them have not seen abject poverty first-hand either in the First or Third Worlds. Conversely, while some GDR citizens admitted a preference to live in a Western country, particularly the FRG, the Netherlands, or one of the Scandinavian countries, I do not recall one instance in which a GDR citizen expressed a preference for capitalism over socialism as a social system. Some GDR citizens seriously questioned whether the GDR had yet achieved socialism and others believed that it had evolved into a "new class society" with the SED elites functioning as a new ruling class.

Many subjects, including SED members, argued that the GDR needed to undergo a process of democratization to achieve authentic or mature socialism. Despite concerted efforts by SED elites and middle-level state functionaries to contain the influence of recent sociopolitical developments in the Soviet Union, most GDR citizens expressed enthusiasm of some degree for the winds of change blowing from the East. Many GDR citizens, particularly members of the intelligentsia, made a distinction between glasnost and perestroika. Many GDR citizens argued that their society needed to undergo a process of glasnost or movement toward socialist democracy, and some even called for authentic party pluralism, ecological sensitivity, and rejection of the productivist ethic. An SED economist told me that the Soviet Union was the only country in Eastern Europe that was moving toward an authentic form of socialism. Conversely, many of my informants expressed mixed feelings about the relevance of perestroika or Soviet-designed economic reforms for the GDR. While admitting that the GDR economy needed to undergo reforms of its own, some argued that the GDR underwent in large measure a type of perestroika in the 1960s and 1970s. Others believed that perestroika may result in growing social stratification in the Soviet Union and "market socialism" similar to that in Yugoslavia and Hungary - countries which they felt faced more severe economic crises than did the GDR.

While open discussion of the sociopolitical developments in the Soviet Union had not yet become part of the public discourse during the period of my stay in the GDR, these developments became increasingly the topics of discussion in lower-level SED meetings, university and college classrooms, work collectives, and non-corporate social networks. On the whole, most GDR citizens appeared to be cautious about the possibilities for significant democratization in their society in the near future. Many argued that much depended on the outcome of new developments in the Soviet Union, and others wondered whether an East German Gorbachev existed somewhere in the Politburo or in the SED elite waiting to assume leadership of the GDR state at the appropriate time.

The Collapse of the German Democratic Republic

The German Democratic Republic, as I experienced it, was a social formation of the past which has been united or, more accurately stated, has been absorbed by the Federal Republic of Germany under the sponsorship of the Christian Democratic Union. Not one of the many people with whom I spoke to during my stay in the GDR expected that their country would embark on the road to unification with the FRG about a year later, although many hoped that the Wall would be dismantled long before the 50- to 100-year period that Erich Honecker predicted that it might have to stand, if necessary, in the supposedly better judgment of the SED leadership. Yet, hindsight now tells us that the GDR stood like a stack of cards, ready to collapse with only the necessary push.

The precipitating factors most immediately responsible for the fall of the GDR lie in the permission that the Soviet Union granted Hungary to open its border with Austria and its policy of desisting from military intervention in Eastern Europe. Once large numbers of GDR citizens, most of them in their 20s and 30s, discovered an escape route to the West through Hungary and later by seeking asylum in FRG embassies in Budapest, Prague, and Warsaw, the seemingly stable GDR economy began to crumble. Another critical moment occurred upon the fortieth anniversary celebration of the GDR on the weekend of 7 October 1989, when Gorbachev responded to the matter of the absence of glasnost and perestroika in the GDR by answering, "He who comes too late will be punished by life itself." As Frank (1990:93) observes, "During his visit to East Germany, Gorbachev literally planted the kiss of death on the cheek of Erich Honecker and then signaled that armed repression of the 9 October rally in Leipzig would be unacceptable." In an effort to stem the tide of the mass exodus to the West and respond to mass demonstrations throughout the GDR, on 18 October 1989 the Politburo replaced the ailing Honecker with his heir-apparent, Egon Krenz, as the General Secretary of the SED. Mass demonstrations opposing Krenz's election forced the Politburo to resign on 7 and 8 November. Hans Modrow, a reform-oriented SED leader from Leipzig, became the First Secretary and announced new travel and emigration regulations, free and secret elections, and a "contractual community" with the FRG. In the euphoria following the opening of the Berlin Wall on 9 November, it appeared for a brief time that the revolution might finally create a socialist democracy in the GDR. A crude poll conducted by an FRG magazine shortly following the opening of the Wall gave the East German Social

Democratic Party (SPD) 20 percent, the West German SPD 15 percent, the New Forum 14 percent, the SED 13 percent, the West German CDU 11 percent, and the East German CDU only 2 percent of the votes in the case of a free election (Minnerup 1989a:7). Indeed, the prevailing mood in the GDR at this point prompted Minnerup (1989b:4) to assert that "so far, the East Germans have shown little appetite for being annexed by the Krupps. A capitalist united Germany is not the inevitable outcome for their revolution against the counterfeit socialism of Ulbricht and Honecker."

> The initial slogans and demands emanating from the streets emphasized democracy, social justice, and an anti-bureaucratic egalitarianism. The GDR's relatively privileged economic position within the Soviet block promised more fertile ground for a socialist reorganization of the economy than the desperate situation confronting the working classes of Poland or Romania. Honecker's destruction of the last remnants of the petit-bourgeoisie and peasantry had theoretically eliminated the social basis of political conservatism. And the explosive growth last fall of groups like "New Forum," "Democracy Now," and the revived Social Democratic Party, all of them anchored in the traditions of the Left, suggested that decaying Stalinism would be superseded by a reinvigorated democratic socialism rather than a headlong rush into D-mark capitalism (Rossman 1990:65).

Although the SED renamed itself the Party of Democratic Socialism, the expression "we are the people" became transformed into "we are one people." Meuschel argues that the roots of this transformation were complex:

> The unrestrained and spontaneous joy that broke out on both sides with the opening of the border doubtlessly strengthened the feeling of togetherness - even if in West Germany the patriotic euphoria has long since sobered into a wary resistance. The sudden possibility of travel to West Germany presented East Germans with the prospect of prosperity they knew from television, but whose scale they could now appreciate. They felt themselves "deceived" by the Party whose domination they had accepted for decades and in which

they had even in part participated. The revelations about corruption (which in fact were not so startling) and the arrest of members of the old elite contributed to repressing the fact there were not, just culprits and victims . . . The slogan "We are one people" also expresses helplessness: the economic infrastructure is antiquated and the social infrastructure is also deteriorating because hundreds of thousands have already left the country and are turning to emigration (Meuschel 1990:22-23).

FRG Chancellor Helmut Koehl capitalized on the mood of the GDR masses and countered Modrow's suggestion of a "contractual community" with a 10 Point Plan for unification of the two Germanies. Apparently Koehl's promise to exchange all GDR savings at one-to-one swayed large numbers of GDR citizens to shift their position on unification. On 18 March 1990, the largest bloc of GDR citizens voted for the rapid unification proposed by the Alliance for Germany, a multi-party coalition led by the East German CDU. Despite the conservative victory, many GDR citizens expressed reservations about full-scale and rapid absorption into the capitalist political economy of the FRG. In East Berlin 35 percent of the electorate voted for the SPD, 30 percent for the Party of Democratic Socialism (PDS), and 6 percent for Alliance 90 (a coalition consisting of New Forum, Democracy Now, and Initiative for Peace and Human Rights). In the southern regions, however, "where about two thirds of the GDR's industrial production originates, but where industrial and environmental neglect has also created the worst desolation, the Right won the critical advantage" (Minnerup 1990:4). Rossman (1990:69) contends that New Forum's reluctance to constitute itself as a political party per se and the collapse of the SED created a political vacuum that FRG and GDR conservative political bodies filled.

After the election, FRG banking interests whittled Koehl's promise down to a one-to-one exchange for the first 4,000 Ostmark of individual adult's savings and two-to-one for everything else, including corporate assets. The euphoria of the Wende, the currency reform in July 1990, and the official unification of the two Germanies in October 1990 wore off quickly for many in East Germany, as we will see in later chapters. Many East Germans found themselves adversely affected by lay-offs resulting from the privatization of former GDR state firms, low wages, rising costs, and cuts in social services. Some East Germans even exclaimed,

"We are a stupid people," as they realized that the newly elected CDU leadership accepted a unification package that would spell economic hardships for many in eastern Germany for some time to come.

Chapter 3

Beyond the Party Line: Why the Construction of Socialism in the German Democratic Republic Failed

The precipitating factors most immediately responsible for the fall of the GDR rest in the permission that the Soviet Union granted Hungary to open its border with Austria and its policy of desisting from military intervention in response to events in Eastern Europe. As Frank (1990:93) observes, "During his visit to East Germany Gorbachev literally planted the kiss of death on the cheek of Erich Honecker and then signaled that armed repression of the 9 October rally in Leipzig would be unacceptable." While recognizing that recent developments in the Soviet Union and Eastern Europe played a significant role in the collapse of the GDR state, I attempt in this chapter to present a broader interpretation why the construction of socialism in the GDR ultimately failed.

As Segall (1983:222) observes, "the concept of socialism is of no use to people seeking solutions within capitalism, but it is essential for those interested to see that system transcended." According to Navarro (1982:80), the "key criterion in defining a social formation as socialist is whether there is control by the working class and its allied forces of the political instance in that formation." From this perspective, the GDR state at the time of its collapse constituted a neo-Stalinist regime which was antithetical to the notion of socialist democracy. While the GDR constitution formally provided for democratic processes in the polity, the work place, and social life, the monopoly of power exercised by SED elites precluded full expression of these ideals in the GDR.

Gregor Gysi, the chairperson of the Party of Democratic Socialism (the successor party of the SED) recognized this in a speech in which he argued,

> GDR society was non-capitalist, but at no time achieved the quality of a socialist society. . . . The means of production were finally, not more highly socialized, because the state property designated as people's property was governed by a centrally organized state, that is, in the last analysis, the man at the head of the party and the state was perhaps the only one who could feel like an owner (Gysi, quoted in *Neues Deutschland,* 16 May 1990).

Factors Impeding the Construction of Socialism in the GDR

A question of greater importance than the actual nature of the GDR is that of why an authoritarian regime continued to exist in the GDR, even after the death of Stalin in 1953 and after it evolved into a relatively, but by no means fully, developed industrial society. In attempting to answer this question, I consider the following external and internal factors that shaped the development of Soviet Zone, and what became in 1949 the GDR, between 1945 and 1989: (1) the Cold War, (2) the revolution from the outside, (3) the economic hardships during the period 1945 to 1961, (4) the contradictions of a productivist-oriented command economy, (5) the hegemony of the capitalist culture of consumption.

The Cold War

A common misconception in the West is the belief that the Soviet Union broke East Germany away from the rest of Germany as a "communist rump state" (Laquer 1985:24). In reality, the partition of Germany occurred in the context of the Cold War which quickly developed between the Western Allies and the Soviet Union after World War II. Stalin wanted to create a buffer zone in Eastern Europe to discourage future invasions of the Soviet Union from Germany or other hostile Western states. While Soviet-sponsored regimes eventually came to power as a result of this policy, Stalin apparently did not believe that Germany as a whole could be simply annexed into the Soviet bloc (Dennis 1988:12). Until at least 1955, the Soviet Union proposed numerous plans that would have resulted in the formation of a reunified, neutral Germany. The USSR made the following proposals in a note delivered to delegates of the three Western powers: (1) that Germany be reestablished as a unified nation within the boundaries created by the Potsdam Conference; (2) that Germany not be required to join any kind of coalition or military alliance directed against any power with which it fought during World War II; (3) that Germany's nonmilitary economy, trade, shipping, and access to world markets not be restricted; and (4) that Germany be allowed the free activity of democratic political parties and organizations (Steiniger 1990:1-2). Vladmir Semenov, the high commissioner in the GDR, "persuaded SED leaders to abandon their policy of 'constructing socialism' initiated in July 1952 and to prepare themselves for loss of power through upcoming reunification under democratic conditions."

Conversely, the United States did not place a priority on the political union of the American, British, French, and Soviet zones but pushed for economic unity and a federal system for the new German state. The French resisted the American effort to strengthen the German economic situation. As early as October 1945 Adenauer declared in an interview with the *News Chronicle* and the Associated Press that the Western Allies should form a Federal Republic on the basis of their zones. In order to pacify France and Belgium, Adenauer suggested the economic integration of West Germany, France, and Belgium. Adenauer eventually had his way within his own party, the Christian Democratic Union (CDU), against strong opposition, and the Americans could thus rely on a good friend for their separatist plans (Thomaneck 1979/80:9-10). In essence, Adenauer believed that neutralization meant Sovietization (Steiniger 1990:97).

At the London Conference, the three Western Allies agreed to a tri-zonal fusion of their respective zones of occupation in a new German federal state. In response to the London Conference of February-March 1948 and the impending currency reform in the Western zones, Soviet Marshall Sokolovsky walked out of the Allied Kommandatura meeting on 20 March 1948. On 7 June 1948 the Western Allies agreed that the their respective occupation zones could draft a constitution for the creation of a new German state. The Western Allies replaced the *Reichmark* with the *Deutschmark* on 18 June 1948. The Ostmarks soon devalued to four or five to one Westmark (Dennis 1988:30). In response to these developments, the Soviets severed all road, rail, and canal links to West Berlin on 24 June 1948. The Berlin Airlift, however, counteracted the Soviet blockade which was discontinued upon agreement of the Four Powers. The German Democratic Republic was formed on 7 October

1949 as a response to the creation of the Federal Republic of Germany on 24 September 1949. The FRG was to speak for all Germans and to be the successor to the Third Reich. Secretary of State John Foster Dulles, who had become a close friend of Konrad Adenauer, promoted the militarization of the FRG.

In 1952 and 1953 the USSR proposed the creation of an all German government in which the FRG and GDR would be granted equal representation and in which each country could determine the means for electing its representatives in part as a measure for deterring the FRG from rearming and entering NATO (Whetten 1980:12). Western Allies proposed in July 1953 a Four Power Conference to discuss free elections and conditions for the creation of a united Germany. The Soviets countered with a more comprehensive plan which sought to ease international tensions between the West and East. The USSR did not formally recognize GDR sovereignty until 1954, and only to a limited degree. Incorporation of the FRG into NATO prompted the USSR to establish full diplomatic relations with the GDR and back its membership in the Warsaw Pact. Nevertheless, the USSR and GDR continued efforts to draw the FRG into some sort of "national compromise" even after the latter joined NATO in 1955. The Four Powers did manage to grant independence to a united neutral Austria at the 1955 Geneva Conference. After 1955 the USSR began to retreat from the option of liquidating the German Democratic Republic in exchange for a unified neutral Germany. Nevertheless, in 1958 Khrushchev proposed that Berlin become a "free city" and that the Allies extend diplomatic recognition to the GDR.

The history of the GDR has been heavily influenced by the presence of its neighbor to the West, namely the FRG – a powerful adversary which openly proclaimed its intention to annihilate the GDR under the banner of *Wiedervereinigung* (reunification). Under the Hallstein Doctrine formulated in the late 1950s, the FRG refused to enter into diplomatic relations with any state, except the USSR, which recognized the GDR. The Hallstein Doctrine in particular effectively inhibited many Third World countries from recognizing the GDR. Although the FRG officially did not grant full diplomatic recognition to the GDR, the *Ostpolitik* of the FRG's Social Democratic Party (SPD) led to a dropping of the Hallstein Doctrine and the partial normalization of relations between the two countries under the provisions of the Basic Treaty (*Grundvertrag*) of 1972. Nevertheless, the FRG never granted full diplomatic recognition to the GDR and viewed all GDR citizens as FRG citizens.

The Revolution from the Outside

The legitimation crisis that the GDR faced since its formation began with the imposition by the Soviet Military Administration District and the Socialist Unity Party (SED) of a Stalinist regime on the East German populace. In the spring of 1945, about 150 key German Communist emigres were assembled in Moscow for a briefing on the political situation and future goals in Germany (McCauley 1979:xiv). On 10 June 1945, the SMAD (Soviet Military Administration in Germany) announced the formation of antifascist parties in the Soviet zone to aid in reconstruction. The reconstituted German Communist Party (KPD) initially did not aim to develop socialism per se, but rather a liberal democratic state. It argued that the premature construction of socialism would threaten the Western Allies and split the zones. In contrast, the Social Democratic Party in the Soviet zone proposed the establishment of a democratic socialist society. The SPD's radical stand apparently contributed to gains in workers' council elections in the late 1945. Furthermore, various leftist groups advocated the establishment of a Soviet German Republic. Indeed, there was a strong inclination on the left and in the antifascist committees to abolish the old parties and create antifascist blocs which would then lead to the formation of a democratic socialist republic (Naimark 1989). The SMAD and the KPD disbanded the leftist sects and antifascist committees because of their spontaneous tendencies. Wolfgang Leonhard (1958) in his memoirs argues that the dissolution of the antifascist committees disrupted the formation of a potentially powerful independent socialist movement in East Germany. Robert Havemann (1972:53), a former SED member and a committed Marxist, notes in his memoirs that the many residents in the town of Spandau shifted their initial support from the KPD to the SPD in the elections of Fall 1946 because they opposed the Soviet domination of East Germany. The KPD had difficulty defending the Soviets right to reparations and its policy of dismantling vital equipment.

A SMAD decree on 10 June 1945 granted permission for the formation of antifascist parties in the Soviet Zone. In April 1946 the KPD and the SPD merged to form the Socialist Unity Party of Germany (SED). Following a brief discussion within the SED of a "German road to socialism," Stalin appointed Walter Ulbricht the General Secretary of the SED. In the course of its evolution into a Soviet-type Marxist-Leninist party, the SED purged its ranks of many former SPD members and Communist advocates of a democratic road to socialism.

The Soviet-model imposed on East Germany provided the SED leadership with an elitist conception of society that was antithetical to notions of both political and economic democracy. Detlef Hermann (1984:129), a former employee of the Institute of International Politics and Economics in East Berlin, contended that SED elites viewed the majority of the populace as still unknowing and believe[d] itself called to enlighten and educate them with every means. Given the high educational level of the GDR populace, this paternalistic attitude produced a deep cynicism of and resentment towards public positions taken by SED elites. At some level, most GDR citizens believed that serious contradictions existed between the ideals and realities of socialism in their country. Efforts on the part of SED elites to suppress information about changes in the USSR during the late 1980s in particular contributed to a legitimation crisis in the GDR, particularly since many of these same elites had pointed for decades to the USSR as the leader of the socialist world. An additional factor contributing to the paternalism of SED elites was the psychology of besiegement that they internalized during the early years of the GDR. As McAdams observes,

> The experience of the 1950s and the 1960s was one which, for many members of the party, confirmed the ethos of militant combat and revolutionary struggle that had already been so much a part of their experience in the Spanish Civil War and the fight against Nazism. Even after the defeat of fascism, the outside world was still regarded as suspect, as full of potential threats to socialist purity. Thus, if the SED were ever to achieve a reconciliation with its surroundings, it was necessary, in the eyes of many party members, for all of those outside elements first to prove that they were no longer threatening and that they accepted the sovereignty of the GDR without reservation (McAdams 1989:19).

Economic Hardships, 1945-1961

The infrastructure of the Soviet Zone and later the GDR had to be reorganized in order to achieve some semblance of self-sufficiency. According to the U.S. *Strategic Bombing Survey*, eastern Germany was not bombed as extensively as the western and southern areas of Germany (cited in Phillips 1986:67-68). The Ruhr drew particularly heavy bombing due to its position in the industrial heartland of Germany. World War II left East Germany with a loss of 15 percent of its productive capacity whereas it left West Germany with a loss of 21 percent of its productive capacity (Childs 1983:22). At the Potsdam Conference, the US calculated that 50 percent of Germany's wealth resided in the Soviet Zone, whereas the Soviets calculated a figure of 42 percent. West Germany retained the major portion of Germany's industry and natural resources, whereas East Germany lacked extensive natural resources and industrial facilities. Furthermore, the Americans were able to recruit a considerable number of key technical specialists away from the Soviet Zone since they first occupied these areas.

At the end of the war, the USSR provided emergency economic aid to the Soviet Zone, despite its own shortages and devastation. In order to develop some semblance of self-sufficiency East Germany constructed steel plants and additional chemical and heavy machinery plants were constructed. Due to these efforts, the Soviet Zone was initially able to recover at a faster rate than the Western zones (Phillips 1986:24-25).

By mid-1948 the production rates of the Western zones overtook that of the Soviet Zone. West Germany received new equipment, raw materials, and food free of charge through the Marshall Plan and other US-aid programs. Between 1948 and 1953, the FRG received a total of $3,298,400,000 in US aid (Radcliffe 1972:115). East Germany did not receive Marshall Plan aid because Stalin viewed it as a devious strategy for extending American capitalist domination over Europe and supporting bourgeois satellites that posed a threat to Soviet security. Conversely, Childs (1983:19) maintains that the U.S. never seriously intended to extend Marshall Plan aid to the Soviet Zone.

Soviet aid was counteracted by war reparations exacted from the Soviet Zone and the GDR during the period 1945 to 1953. Twenty-six percent of the infrastructure in East Germany was dismantled as opposed to 12 percent of that in West Germany (McAdams 1985:35-36). In addition to dismantling factories, railroad tracks, mining installations, and other equipment, the Soviets sent East German workers to the USSR for extended work projects. The SMAD also formed Soviet companies (SAGs), two-thirds of which were initially enterprises designated for dismantling (McCauley 1979:7). During their period of operation the SAGs accounted for about a third of the East German industrial output, only about a third of which remained in East Germany. Except for a uranium operation at Wismut, all of the SAGs were sold back to the GDR by 1954 for approximately 5 billion Marks. In May 1946 General Lucius Clay ordered the cessation of reparation payments to the USSR from the American Zone. East Germany paid the USSR an estimated $19 billion in reparations whereas total Soviet aid to that country during the period 1945 to 1960 came to an estimated $9.4 billion, including reparations cancellations (Phillips 1986:160). According to one source, reparations accounted for 33 percent of the Soviet Zone's GNP in 1947 (Childs 1983:70). The bulk of Soviet aid came in the aftermath of the workers' rebellion in the GDR in June 1953. The glamour of the West German economic miracle, the harsh economic conditions in the GDR, and the repressive policies of the GDR state prompted approximately three million people, roughly one-sixth of East Germany's population, to emigrate between 1945 and 1961 to the FRG. According to Ardaugh,

> Half of those who left were under 25, while the older ones included many thousands of engineers, doctors and other specialists who were vital to the GDR. The country was bleeding to death; and it was braindrain above all that in August 1961 led Ulbricht, with Moscow's backing, to build the Wall and so block the easy escape route via West Berlin. It was an ignominious confession of failure, and Ulbricht is said to have admitted later, in private, that it was his greatest defeat in the propaganda battle to prove the worth of the GDR (Ardaugh 1987:324-325).

While the Wall violated the human rights of GDR citizens, it served to stabilize the GDR economy for the next 28 years.

Contradictions of the Command, 1961 to 1989

After the construction of the Berlin Wall in 1961 and several years of consolidation, the GDR embarked upon a period of impressive economic growth. The GDR experimented with economic reforms during this period, implementing the New Economic System in 1963 under which state enterprises were allocated some decision-making responsibility and profit was identified as a key economic lever. The Seventh Party Congress in 1967 initiated the Economic System of Socialism which attempted to incorporate cybernetics, systems theory, and computer science into the planning process. In 1971 the Honecker regime announced its commitment to the "principal task" of the economy, namely the enhancement of the material and social needs of the GDR people.

During the 1960s, the GDR underwent a "red economic miracle" during which it became the most affluent society within COMECON (Council of Mutual Economic Assistance). World Bank figures listed the GDR in tenth place among industrial countries in 1980. During the turndown in the West German "economic miracle" around 1966-1967, the GDR reportedly enjoyed a higher rate of economic growth at around 5 percent annually than the FRG (McAdams 1985:5). The average monthly income of a worker increased from 558 Ostmarks in 1960s to 1,140 Ostmarks in 1985 (Burrant 1988:88-89). As of the early 1980s, food prices had remained frozen for more than a decade, and rents were set at extremely low levels. In 1983 the state spent over 12 million Marks in food subsidies and during the period 1980 through 1983 rent subsidies averaged 8.3 million Marks per year. GDR agriculture generally fed the population at an adequate level, although fresh fruits and various vegetables were generally in short supply.

Gorbachev and other Soviet officials often looked at the GDR economic system for clues as to how to reform the Soviet economy. Goldman (1987:167) admits that "it is hard to tell whether what has happened in East Germany is due to the fact that German workmanship is involved, or that the East Germans have discovered a way of making central planning work." In the late 1960s, the GDR began to form *Kombinate*, groupings of related enterprises. By 1986, 132 Kombinate, with an average of 25,000 workers for each, existed at the national level and 93 existed at the regional level.

Despite the GDR economic miracle, the command economy contained a number of glaring contradictions. Supply shortages, cautious managerial policies, and an 8.75 hour work day produced low worker motivation. According to Schnitzer (1972:363), "although relatively more persons are employed in industry in the GDR, net per capita output in 1967 was 83 percent of that of the FRG." He calculated that labor productivity in the GDR was at one third less than that in the FRG. The first Five Year Plan (1951 to 1955) demonstrated that the GDR economy suffered from an over-concentration of decision-making and administration.

During the 1970s and 1980s, the GDR increasingly imported sophisticated technology from advanced capitalist countries, particularly the FRG - a practice which further exacerbated the drive for hard currency and the economic dependency of the GDR on the capitalist world-system. Despite its limited energy resources, the GDR had been able to cover 65 percent of its energy requirements from domestic sources, a condition similar to that of most Western industrial nations (Scharf 1984:87). In 1985 lignite or brown coal supplied approximately 72 percent of the GDR's domestic energy needs (Gates 1988:137). Unfortunately, an inferior technology resulted in severe industrial pollution and considerable wastage of energy sources, evidenced by the fact that the per capita consumption of primary energy was 18 percent higher in the GDR than in the FRG during 1975. Most of the GDR's imported raw materials and energy resources came from the USSR and Eastern Europe.

The 1973 oil price explosion and the world wide recession of the late 1970s adversely affected the GDR economy. As early as 1970, the GDR began to show a trade deficit with the West and after 1975 with the USSR (Gates 1988:133-134). The USSR had been increasingly reluctant to deliver ever greater quantities of raw materials to the GDR because it could sell them on the world market for higher prices and hard currency (Stahnke 1983). The increasing cost of domestic energy extraction and imported energy resources, the export of higher quality consumer items to the West (in order to obtain hard currency and to pay debts to Western banks), and the heavy state subsidies for housing, basic food products, and social services began to erode the relatively high material standard of living that GDR citizens had come to accept as their due.

The Hegemony of the Capitalist Culture of Consumption

Throughout their existence, most post-revolutionary societies embarked upon a process of industrialization in order to improve the material living standards of their populaces and to develop a military force capable of counteracting hostile actions by advanced capitalist societies. Undoubtedly, the invasion of the USSR by Great Britain, France, the United States, Czechoslovakia, Japan, and ten other countries during the civil war period of 1918 through 1920 convinced the Bolsheviks that they needed to rapidly industrialize their country, even if it required repressive measures. Under these conditions, the principle of the "dictatorship of the proletariat" became transformed into democratic centralism, and in turn into the dictatorship of the party and, under Stalin, the dictatorship of one man. At the cost of millions of lives, the Stalinist command economy propelled the Soviet Union from a largely underdeveloped agrarian nation into an industrial nation. The devastation of World War II and the US nuclear arms build-up after the war undoubtedly contributed to Stalin's perception that the USSR remained a besieged nation. The command economy elevated the Warsaw Pact to near parity with NATO, but also left glaring gaps in the availability of consumer goods. While this has been especially true for the USSR, the arms race had placed a serious strain on the GDR's economy as well. In 1987 the FRG and the GDR spent $34,130 million and $14,440 million, respectively, on military expenditures (U.S. Arms Control and Disarmament Agency 1988). Whereas military expenditures constituted 3.0 percent of the FRG's GNP, they constituted 7.3 percent of the GDR's GNP. In the case of East Germany, Stalin promoted contradictory programs of de-industrialization, namely in the form of reparations, and re-industrialization. The workers' rebellion of 1953 convinced the Soviets and SED elites that they must more effectively fulfill consumer demands. The West German economic miracle of the 1950s continued to prompt many GDR citizens to flee to the other Germany. After the erection of the Wall in 1961, SED elites attempted to appease the GDR populace with "consumer socialism."

Nonetheless, most GDR citizens continued to be affected by the hegemony of the capitalist culture of consumption, which they learned about vis-a-vis the FRG media, although in a rather glamorized form, and eventually through contacts with relatives in the FRG. As in other post-revolutionary states, the GDR state's effort to "catch up with the West" by providing its populace with an ever growing array of consumer products strained the capacity of the infrastructure to the limits, resulting in increasing environmental degradation. At the same time, the GDR state attempted to suppress environmentalists as well as reformed-minded SED members who called into question the rationality of the culture of consumption. SED elites themselves, with their Volvos and privileged access to other Western products, led the way in emulating the culture of consumption. Unlike the FRG, the GDR lacked extensive access to the cheap resources and labor of southern Europe and the Third World that played a significant role in subsidizing the West German culture of consumption. As Peter Marcuse aptly observes,

> West Germany, Sweden, and the United States produce as efficiently as they do in part because they benefit from an international division of labor. If the capitalist standard of living were calculated on a comprehensive basis, it would have to include Haiti as well as Switzerland, Ethiopia as well as England, the underpaid and repressed millions of Korea, as well as the overpaid few of Wall Street (Marcuse 1990b:51).

Chapter 4

Life Inside the Socialist Unity Party of Germany (SED)

Most accounts of the Socialist Unity Party of Germany focus on the inner workings of the party based upon official party documents as well as the policies and actions of SED elites, particularly General Secretaries (namely Walter Ulbricht and Erich Honecker), the Politburo, and the Central Committee. This chapter attempts to provide new insights into the SED and East Germany both before and after unification by focusing on the experiences of several individuals who were either rank-and-file members of the party or held lower-echelon positions of leadership within it (Also see Hermann 1984). In order to set the context for my subjects, I present a discussion of the structure of the SED.

The Social Structure of the SED

Unlike the one-party system that existed prior to perestroika in the former Soviet Union, the GDR had five political parties. The SED was established in 1946 as a merger of the German Communist Party and the Social Democratic Party in the Soviet Zone of Germany. It functioned as the ruling party from the creation of the GDR in 1949 until the days of the Wende in the fall of 1989 and the winter of 1990. Despite the existence of four other parties, political pluralism was more a matter of form than substance in the GDR since the non-ruling parties, which were organized into the National Front along with several other national organizations, acquiesced to the SED leadership on most matters and therefore had no clear-cut identity within the GDR state.

The GDR state inherited its Leninist party structure from the Soviet Union. Although Lenin himself encouraged free and open debate within the Communist Party, his concern about the difficult political and economic situation prompted him to call a ban on factionalism within the party as an emergency measure until the victory of the revolutionary was ensured. As John Ehrenberg observes:

> Lenin acknowledged, the "dictatorship of the proletariat" might boil down to the dictatorship of its politically organized minority. But while he affirmed this "in general," he was careful to note that the dictatorship of the proletariat must be carried out by a party which is accountable to the workers through the democratic soviets. . . The soviet republic remained the instrumentality through which the workers' party could organize the proletarian dictatorship - even if it was not yet clear how the nonparty workers would supervise its work (Ehrenberg 1992:159).

External and internal factors ultimately prevented the creation of democracy in any form, centralized or otherwise, in the Soviet Union and ultimately contributed to the emergence of bureaucratic centralism, particularly under Stalin but also under his successors. The grim realities of economic, political, and social life in the Soviet Union must be placed within a larger context, namely, the fact that socialist-oriented revolutions occurred in the periphery rather than in the core capitalist nations and also the response of the advanced capitalist countries to these revolutions. According to Foster:

> From the moment of its emergence in the October Revolution of 1917 - occurring in the midst of World War I - the Soviet Union was faced with the enmity of the advanced capitalist world. It was not until after World War II, however, that conflict took center stage in world history. Under U.S. leadership the West sought to isolate the U.S.S.R. and to push back revolutionary forces throughout the third world. Both the United States and the Soviet Union thus became involved in a global arms race that consumed vast economic and environmental resources (Foster 1994:56).

In addition to the stifling influence that capitalist encirclement placed on the development of democratic processes in the Soviet Union, one must take into consideration the fact that it inherited or modified authoritarian structures from the preceding Czarist state. As Schwartz (1991:68) observes, "In an isolated and relatively backward country, lacking strong democratic traditions, and where a militant but extremely small working class had been decimated by civil war, the bureaucracy was able to impose Stalinism as a noncapitalist crash modernization programme."

The SED was organized on the basis of the Leninist principle of "democratic centralism" under which open discussion of issues was to occur prior to centralized coordination of decision-making at the various levels of the party. In ascending importance, the levels of the SED included the *Grundorganization* or basic organization (generally organized at the workplace), the *Kreis* (district) organization, the *Bezirk* (regional) organization, and the central party organization (Dennis 1988). At the level of the central party organization, the Party Congress, which was held every five years, elected the Central Committee. As theoretically the highest organ of the SED, the Central Committee elected the General Secretary and the Politburo, which included representatives from the Ministry of Defense, the Ministry of State Security, the Free German Youth, and the *Freier Deutscher Gewerkschaftsbund* (Free German Trade Union Association). In theory, the *Volkskammer* (People's Parliament), which included representatives from the five political parties and four mass organizations represented in a unitary list determined by the National Front, served as the supreme organ of state power in the GDR. In reality, the Politburo as a self-perpetuating body made the ultimate decisions on virtually every formal aspect of social life in the SED and the GDR. Steele describes the SED Politburo in the following terms:

> The Politburo still follows the tight-lipped conspiratorial traditions of the days in opposition and the underground. All decisions are taken at the top and there is minimal public or press discussion of them. Under the principle of democratic centralism decisions are passed down the line to the central committee and local party organizations for implementation (Steele 1977:143).

The SED elite consisted of two broad categories: (1) the leading cadres who had risen in the party apparatus and carried out "almost exclusively political leadership and control functions in the Politburo, the Secretariat of the Central Committee, or Secretariats of the SED Bezirk executives" and (2) the leading functionaries and party experts in "the state apparatuses, economy, agriculture, mass organizations, and military and cultural elites" who functioned in some ways as an "institutionalized counter elite" (Ludz 1972:67). As Baylis (1974:x) observes, "the creation of a technical intelligentsia is a part of a larger process of the manipulation of social structure by a self-conscious political elite which sees itself as a revolutionary vanguard engaged in the task of creating a radically better society."

In essence, SED elites stifled any semblance of democratic election to higher party organs by drawing up most of the lists of candidates and by closely regulating the electoral process. As Kurt Sontheimer and William Bleek (1975) note, the party leadership determined the fundamental political rulings. After Stalin's death, SED party life took on more an ethos of consultative authoritarianism as opposed to absolute dictatorship. While no Gulag camps per se existed or mass executions occurred in the GDR, the seeming omnipresence of the Stasi reinforced antidemocratic patterns.

Members of the Politburo lived in relative luxury in a compound called Wandlitz located north of Berlin and increasingly became isolated from the realities of social life in the GDR. Although by Western standards the social amenities enjoyed by the Politburo and other SED elites were relatively modest compared to those of corporate owners and executives and many politicians in the West, many East Germans saw the lifestyles of the leaders of their state as a violation of socialist ideals whereas others were more offended by their paternalistic posture toward the masses. In a somewhat similar vein, Paul Gleye argues,

> The Upper 10,000 were widely known to live lavishly, but even so it was a modest lavishness compared with that of Third-World dictators. It was also generally believed that these people were provided things such as fruits and vegetables delivered to their opulent homes in Volvograd. Such abuses were indeed revealed after the fall of the communist government, but among all of the country's problems they were not considered major. When, on the other hand, at the end of 1989 East Germans learned of the private hunting preserves of the top leaders, they were incensed. I, on the other hand, could not but reflect on the tameness of such excesses (Gleye 1991:197).

Although executives in the central state apparatus were increasingly professionally trained, the social composition of the SED itself retained a largely proletarian complexion. In 1966 45.6 percent of its members were blue-collar workers, 6.4 percent cooperative farmers, 12.3 percent intelligentsia, 16.1 percent white-collar employees, 1.6 percent students and pupils, 0.7 tradespeople and government-supported businesspeople, 4.4 percent housewives, and 12.1 percent pensioners (Ludz 1972:179). In that same year, 26.5 percent of SED members were women (Ludz 1972:184).

Life in the GDR and the SED

The former SED members who served as my subjects in essence constituted voices with whom I entered into what Kevin Dwyer (1979) terms a "dialogic" relationship. While I became acquainted with many SED members during my Fulbright Lectureship in 1988-1989, I developed a particularly close relationship with Walter Rusch and Petra Preussler, both of whom have given me permission to use their actual names. I refer to my other subjects who were SED members by pseudonyms.

In 1988-1989, Walter taught in the department of ethnography at Humboldt University and Petra taught English classes at an *Oberschule* (school for grades 1-10) in East Berlin. I met them several times again during 1991, first on my sabbatical in the spring semester and also while in Berlin as a participant in a German Studies summer seminar sponsored by the Fulbright Commission. I had an opportunity to briefly visit Petra once again in early June 1992. Most recently I met both Walter and Petra during the summer of 1995. In addition to representing different genders, Walter and Petra represent different generations in the history of the GDR. Walter was born in 1936, grew up in Nazi Germany, and witnessed the development of the GDR over the course of its forty year history. Petra represents the first generation of East Germans who spent their entire lives, at least prior to the unification of 1990, as GDR citizens.

Walter's Life in the German Democratic Republic

Because his father was a teacher, the first years of Walter's life were spent living in the house reserved for the school teacher of a small village in Mecklenburg. When the Soviet army occupied the village in May 1945, he felt hatred toward the soldiers because his father had died fighting in Russia. In mid-1946 Walter moved with his mother, brother, and sister into a room in his father's mother's house in Wismar, a Hanseatic city on the Baltic Sea. While studying for his *Abitur* (high school examination), he became very involved with a folk dance ensemble, which consisted largely of the children of shipyard workers. His classmates ridiculed him for associating with their social inferiors and attempted to persuade him to attend church activities with them. Given that his mother had never taken him to church, Walter avoided contact with his classmates because they opposed the GDR's social system and socialized primarily in their religious congregations.

Although Walter was a member of the Young Pioneers and the Free German Youth, these organizations did not have any special political significance for him since they seemed like a normal part of growing up in the GDR. Shortly after he was inducted into the army in September 1955, a political officer ordered Walter to join the SED because he had completed his Abitur. He told himself that he would never join a political party with such arrogant people. After completion of his military duty, he began his studies in ethnography at Humboldt University. As a student, Walter became more interested in political affairs and was even arrested for pamphleteering for the SED during a West Berlin election campaign. Despite his commitment to socialist ideals, he was rejected for membership in the SED in 1961 because as a "workers' and peasants' party" it maintained a quota on the number of intellectuals admitted. After obtaining his *Diplom* (university undergraduate diploma) in 1961, Walter became an *Aspirant* (graduate student) and finally was allowed to join the SED in 1963.

Walter interrupted his dissertation work on the nature of the pre-colonial Buganda state in 1965 when he took a position with the League for People's Friendship in the GDR's cultural center in Zanzibar, the first capitalist country to have extended diplomatic recognition to the GDR. According to Barnett (1992:102), "East Germany's diplomatic offensive of the late 1960s was specifically aimed at drumming up Third World support for its goal of international diplomatic recognition." At any rate, Walter became the director of the center in 1966 and worked in that capacity until 1971. His work involved frequent trips to other African countries, including Somalia, Ethiopia, Senegal, Ghana, Sierra Leone, Zambia, and the Tanzanian mainland after Zambia was incorporated as Zanzibar into the United Republic of Tanzania. While Walter worked in Africa, various diplomats from the Federal Republic of

Germany tried to persuade Walter to defect by offering him a position as a Dozent. In 1969 the FRG dropped the Hallstein Doctrine, under which the FRG refused diplomatic recognition of any country, other than the Soviet Union, that recognized the GDR. Following this shift in policy, members of the FRG diplomatic corps made concerted efforts to work in cooperation with their GDR counterparts.

In 1971 Walter returned to East Berlin where he continued to work for the Liga and resumed work on his doctoral dissertation, which he defended in 1973. In 1974 he joined the ethnography faculty at Humboldt University. In 1976, he, with Lothar Stein, conducted six months of ethnographic research on the integration of the Bedouins and oasis peasants of Siwa in the western Egyptian desert. In 1978 Walter, again with Professor Stein, was involved in an effort to establish a national museum in Khartoum, the capital of the Sudan. Due to a lack of funds, the project fell through but eventually was carried out with aid from the FRG. In 1976 Walter spent a half a year conducting archival research in Tanzania. As a result of his many publications on African cultures, the GDR state permitted him to attend many scholarly conferences in the West.

Prior to the unification, Walter said that he always held SED leadership positions of one sort or another at the ground level while he was on the faculty at the university. SED members were required to regularly attend three monthly Monday evening meetings - that of the *Parteigruppe* (party group), the *Grundorganization* (ground organization), and the *Parteilehrjahr* (the party study year). At the university, the ethnography sub-department, which was a part of the history department, made decisions regarding its own day-to-day operations, as long as it conformed with the regulations of higher governing bodies. The Parteigruppe also spent much time discussing recommendations made by higher governing bodies, such as the SED leadership, the university's party secretary, or the Rektor of the university. At this level, particularly in institutions of higher education, considerable debate could take place, especially in the final years of the GDR. In carrying out his responsibility as Parteigruppe secretary, Walter always reported that the majority of members were in agreement with the recommendation but never specified who had objected to it. On various occasions, Walter also served as the secretary of the Parteilehrjahr which occurred every four years. The ground organizations elected delegates for the Bezirk (district) administration, which in turn elected delegates for the *Parteitag* (party conference) at which they would listen to discussions of plans that the SED leadership had made for the next four years.

Walter said that there was a time when hardly anyone dared ask questions in a Parteigruppe meeting. Because dissenters often were criticized, either publicly or in reports, he said that he refrained from questioning recommendations that came from above. Walter stated, "I was convinced that I had to fulfill the goals of the party. The party overruled my own views." In order to carry out the party's goals, he sometimes found ways to circumvent its rigid structure. A high-ranking GDR diplomat to Tanzania told Walter that he must cease visiting the new secretary of state, a long-time personal friend, in his home as he had been doing on a weekly basis because it would be a violation of protocol, but his friend, the General Consul, told him to discreetly maintain his informal contacts with his old student colleague.

Petra's Life in the GDR

Like Walter, Petra also was a staunch SED member who was devoted to socialist ideals and the development of the GDR. During the GDR era, she was a very popular teacher whose pupils nick-named her *Rotkaeppchen* (Red Riding Hood) for her political zeal. In contrast to Walter, leadership was thrust upon her more by default rather than by advancing along regular channels. As Duncan Smith reports, SED leadership appears to have been a precondition for holding positions of leadership in GDR schools:

> All staff members are required to attend the *Parteilehrtage* (SED informational meetings) which are conducted on the first Monday of every month. The SED chapter meets in closed session on a weekly basis, but this monthly meeting is open to all staff, and they are required to come (Smith 1988:16).

Unlike her father, who staunchly supported most of the policies of the SED leadership, Petra was a maverick both in and outside of the SED. Indeed, generational gaps developed in the SED with younger members becoming more reform-oriented. While Petra never belonged to any of the small underground reform groups that existed within the SED, it is important to note that most of the leading critics in the GDR emerged from the ranks of the SED. The League of Democratic Communists came out of the closet in 1977 calling for extensive reforms in the SED, including the abandonment of the notion of democratic centralism, the creation of a pluralist state with an independent parliament and judiciary, and the abolition of a privileged party elite as well as wage differentials between managers and workers.

At any rate, Petra grew up in Rostock, a Hanseatic city and the major East German port on the Warnow River which flows into the Baltic Sea. Because her parents worked as journalists in various countries, including Sweden and Argentina, she attended a boarding school for many years. After the completion of her Abitur, she studied language teaching in German and English at Humboldt University. Petra taught English to pupils at what formerly was an Oberschule in the Lichtenberg area of East Berlin. She lived with a Swedish worker, whom she met while he was on a construction project in the GDR, for seven years and had a son with him. When he decided to return to Sweden, Petra chose to remain in the GDR and raise her son alone. She finds most East German men to be jealous types and thus finds herself more attracted to foreign men. Although she is an attractive and intelligent woman, she refers to herself as a *komische Nudel* (funny noodle) who does not wish to live in a permanent relationship with a man. Petra resides with her eleven-year old son in a modest apartment in Lichtenberg. Before the unification, Petra described GDR women as *selbstbewusst* (self-aware) and economically independent of men. This is in keeping with Peter Marcuse's (1991:272) observation that in the GDR "women's rights, in particular to abortion, child care, and parenting leaves and time off, were stronger than in West Germany." Petra joined the SED while she was a university student and served as the school party secretary for several years, a position that she ironically obtained as a result of her critical views on SED dogmatism rather than conformity to party discipline. Although she was never expelled from the SED for her views, Petra believes that she was transferred to new schools as a punishment for expressing them in party meetings, faculty meetings, and in the classroom. Whereas the school administration claimed that her first transfer was necessary because of a decline in enrollment, she maintains that her contacts with foreigners, including her Swedish common-law husband, and her support for the Solidarity movement in Poland were the real causes for it. At her second school, she questioned the expectation that all pupils belong to the Free German Youth. While nomination to a study place in a *Parteischule* (party school) was generally considered an honor for dedicated SED members exhibiting leadership potential, the director used it as a strategy to get rid of a dissident voice on her faculty. Nevertheless, because of her avid interest in politics, which she regards to be her hobby, Petra accepted the nomination in order to further her own understanding of Marxist-Leninist theory.

Upon completion of her one-year study at the party school, she received a transfer to a third school. The school administration told her that she would have to serve as the school party secretary because she had attended a party school. According to Smith (1988:69), the chapter party secretary was expected to reveal to "those present the substance of party politics and . . . to discuss with all those attending any specific or general issues." Rather than accepting the widespread policy of appointing people to positions of leadership, Petra questioned how she could serve in such an important position without her colleagues knowing very much about her. She also argued her selection by the administration would be undemocratic and gave five speeches before her colleagues calling for the election of the party secretary. The administration finally gave into her demands for an election after two months. Petra maintains that she was the sole candidate because none of her colleagues desired the position since it entails a great deal of work. Although party reports ordinarily presented a glowing account of the collective's activities, Petra reported upon the problems in her school. She suspects that these portions of her reports were not mentioned in the Kreis (circle) report forwarded to the Bezirk (district) office, which in turn submitted a report to the Central Committee of the activities of all the party collectives in East Berlin. On the whole, Petra believes that party functionaries, contrary to the principles of socialist democracy, suppressed dissenting opinions within the SED and reported what they thought the Central Committee wanted to hear.

Views of the SED Leadership and the GDR

Prior to the unification, as long as Walter can remember, he regarded socialism to be a better system than capitalism. He was aware that many people in the FRG lived at a higher material standard of living than in the GDR. For example, as a university student, he ate a large meal almost every week at his aunt's and uncle's home in West Berlin and could clearly see that they lived at a higher material standard of living than most East Germans. Conversely, he recognized that many West Germans did not live as well as his uncle and aunt. Furthermore, his travels in Africa allowed him to witness first hand the victims of Western colonialism and neocolonialism. Although he had many opportunities to flee to the West both prior to the construction of the Wall in 1961 and afterwards, he always chose to return to the GDR because he believed that its ideology was superior to capitalism. Walter lamented that the SED had within its ranks careerists and opportunists, but he believed that they were in the minority. His observation concurs with Smith's remarks about the spectrum of attitudes held by SED members:

> In the ranks of the . . . party are careerists, opportunists, perhaps cynics, and the like . . . But it would, in my opinion, be a great misunderstanding of another reality of really existing socialism to regard the SED in this manner or to make it the equivalent of a "bunch of careerists and opportunists." There are, of course, true believers, the so-called "two hundred percenters." (Smith 1988:81).

Unfortunately, the "true believers," the careerists, and the opportunists appear to have dominated the highest leadership positions in the SED. Walter now believes that they contributed heavily to the collapse of the GDR. Walter also regrets that the SED had within its ranks dogmatic members who did much to impair the construction of socialism. One of the turning points in his life occurred after the Soviet invasion of Czechoslovakia in 1968. Prior to a visit from his supervisor from East Berlin, he had heard only rumors about what had occurred in Czechoslovakia. When Walter asked his Chef about recent events there, the latter angrily retorted, "Are you a Communist or not? Did you need a rationale for what occurred?" This incident permanently strained Walter's relationship with his Chef, even after he had left the Liga. Walter never doubted the concept of socialism, but over the course of his lifetime he came to question the sincerity of certain SED members, Unfortunately, he feels that it was easier for dogmatic members to advance up the ranks of the SED than open-minded ones.

During his student days, Walter said that Walter Ulbricht, the General Secretary of the SED, was like a god for him and his fellow classmates. They only criticized leaders in their immediate circle. When the Politburo replaced Ulbricht with Erich Honecker as the General Secretary of the SED in 1971, Walter accepted it as a normal course of action, given Ulbricht's age. In contrast to Ulbricht, perhaps in part because he had matured, he did not have strong feelings one way or another about Honecker as a personality. Prior to Honecker's promotion, Walter knew of him only as a SED functionary who served as the Chairperson of the FDJ. Walter stated, "The party was the party and not Honecker. I served the party and not Honecker." Despite his dedication to the SED, he did not always agree with its policies. He opposed the decision of the SED leadership in October 1988 to ban the circulation of *Sputnik,* a popular Soviet magazine, in the GDR. Walter recognizes that the Leninist principle of democratic centralism, in which discussion about policies theoretically flowed both up and down the party hierarchy, was not existent in the SED. Conversely, he generally did not question the decisions made by the SED leadership because he believed that they had an overview of the entire GDR society. He said that rank-and-file members and members in lower-level leadership positions, such as himself, were merely expected to carry out the decisions made by higher-echelon SED leaders. Walter admitted that he never questioned the GDR electoral system while he was a SED member, adding that the decisions in many so-called democratic elections in the West are predetermined through the process of candidate selection. He now believes that bureaucratic centralism was the major reason that the GDR collapsed. Walter stated, "More or less, every comrade knew that something was wrong, but most comrades, including myself, did nothing about it. We accepted it, while saying that a lot was *Mist* (dung)." Prior to the unification, while recognizing that the GDR needed to undergo certain economic reforms, he felt that the perestroika debate was much more relevant for the Soviet Union than the GDR because of the former's greater economic underdevelopment.

Although Walter still believes in the ideals of socialism, he now feels that the construction of socialism to date has not been possible due to the conditions, both internal and external, that the Soviet Union, the GDR, and other Eastern-bloc nations faced. He said that he didn't realize before the Wende that SED elites enjoyed so many privileges. Walter is not sure whether the achievement of an authentic form of democratic socialism will ever occur, but if it does, it may require another 200 or 300 years. Walter feels that the short history of the GDR demonstrates the impossibility of developing socialism in the present historical epoch. He fears that the possible reemergence of a neo-Stalinist dictatorship in the USSR would even further damage the socialist vision. He feels that human societies throughout the world must for the immediate future find a middle way between capitalism in its starkest forms and the concept of socialism, perhaps welfare capitalism such as exists in Sweden. Walter feels that most young people were unaware of the sacrifices that older generations of East Germans had to make in order to help the GDR achieve its social benefits and international status as an industrial society and development force in certain parts of the Third World.

If indeed many young East Germans did take for granted what they had inherited from their parents and grandparents, Petra was not one of them. Conversely, she criticized the consumerism of many East Germans and pointed with pride to her economic self-sufficiency as a single mother in the GDR. When her son was a youngster, he underwent three months of state-paid therapy at a children's sanatorium for a stuttering problem. She received a 300 Mark clothing allowance for her son and funds to visit him once during the course of his therapy. The GDR paid a total of 5,000 Marks for Petra's son's stay in the sanatorium. Petra feels that if more East Germans had been able to travel to the West prior to the Wende, many would have appreciated the social benefits that they enjoyed. She laments that the East German masses had lacked motivation and failed to take initiative in their work, but acknowledges that these patterns, along with their avid consumerism, may have been a consequence of their alienation in the workplace and lack of control over the means of production.

While Petra felt that the GDR had already undergone a process of perestroika, she argued that it needed to undergo glasnost. Prior to the Wende, Petra criticized the Politburo for being too set in its ways and the media for presenting a distorted image of GDR social life. After the Wende, she stated that the SED leadership had created a dictatorship, not a socialist democracy, and that the Stasi constituted a state within a state.

The Experiences of Other Party Members Within the SED

In this section I discuss the experiences of several other SED members. I met some of them several times on various occasions and met others only once or twice. While each of their experiences within the SED are unique, they also exhibit certain parallels with those of Walter and Petra that reveal the inner workings of the SED.

Heinrich's Story

Heinrich, whom I interviewed in early 1991 and who died sometime thereafter, was reared in a Catholic working-class family in Munich and received training as a *Maurer* (bricklayer). Because he was unemployed in 1929, he considered immigrating to the United States. Instead Heinrich acted in 1931 upon his convictions as a member of the German Communist Party (KPD) by taking a position in a German building brigade in the Soviet Union. He met Nikita Khrushchev while supervising construction work in 1937 at the Soviet Institute for Experimental Medicine. Unfortunately, between 1935 and 1938 Stalin ordered the arrest of all German, Polish, and Czech guest workers on the charge of being spies and counter-revolutionaries. Heinrich said that ordinary workers received prison terms of five to ten years and worker supervisors, such as himself, received terms of 25 years. An East German publication reports the names of 1,136 Germans who were imprisoned by Stalin during the 1930s (*In den Fangen des KKWD* 1991). In reality, Heinrich believed that the actual figure of German prisoners was considerably higher in that only two of the forty members of his work brigade are listed in this report. He lost his job in 1937 and served a prison sentence from 1938 to 1956. Because his German wife mysteriously disappeared, Heinrich married a Russian engineer in 1956. Despite his bitter experiences as a political prisoner in the Soviet Union, Heinrich never gave up his socialist ideals. Conversely, he felt that Stalin pushed the development of socialist democracy back 100 years. He said that in 1932-1933 many of the German workers who returned from the Soviet Union told stories about the privileges of the *nomenklatura*, the bureaucrats, and the intellectuals there which turned many other German workers toward fascism. Heinrich received an amnesty in 1956 and immigrated to the GDR a couple of years later in order to help to build socialism in a section of his native land.

Whereas he felt that Wilhelm Pieck was a good leader, Heinrich maintained that Walter Ulbricht was a bad one. Because of his position as a supervisor for the Stasi, he became acquainted with many of its employees, including Marcus Wolf, the head of foreign espionage. Wolf arranged a meeting for Heinreich to voice his complaints about the inefficiencies of the GDR economy before the Central Committee (ZK). When he told the ZK that there was need for more manual work and less paper work in the GDR, Heinrich stated that the ZK dismissed his complaint by noting that RIAS - a FRG television channel - had made similar propagandistic accusations. He felt that the GDR would have developed a more efficient economy than the FRG if it had fired all of its inefficient managers and bureaucrats. He argued that instead the Politburo leaders and Stasi chiefs went on hunting expeditions, developed inflated egos, and became estranged from the workers. Heinrich criticized the Stasi for having failed to report on the economic inefficiencies in the GDR. Although he felt that the GDR provided many significant social benefits for its citizens, he complained about the poor conditions and the shortage of nurses in the nursing homes. While on a trip following the Wende, he was amazed by the cleanliness of Munich and the variety of sausages available in its shops. Heinrich cried and asked himself, "Why could we have not done the same in the GDR?"

Michael's Story

When I met Michael in early October 1988, he had been working for the past several years for the League for People's Friendship but was about to take a position conducting historical research at a historical research institute. Given that he worked for a propaganda arm of the GDR state, I was surprised as to how critical he was of the SED leadership and the GDR state. Michael was quite excited about glasnost and perestroika in the Soviet Union and noted that the GDR needed a more democratic leadership.

At our first meeting, Michael referred to some of the information disseminated abroad by the Liga as propaganda and added that many GDR citizens didn't believe much of the information disseminated by the GDR state in the mass media. He said that he relied on a combination of information from the GDR, FRG, and other news sources as well as periodic visits to the United States to provide him with a picture of social reality in the world. When we met again in early 1991, he stated that the Liga provided positions for SED members who could not obtain positions in the diplomatic service or in the upper echelons of the Party. He maintained that the Liga had some naive leaders who believed that they would be able to recruit Communists in foreign countries simply by extolling the wonders of GDR society.

Michael was not quite sure how the SED elites made decisions, but he felt that the Politburo ultimately made all important decisions. In his view, the Liga's representative on the ZK didn't seem to know what was going on in the government. Michael stated that many GDR citizens did not regard Honecker to be a particularly poor leader, but believed that his advisors were stupid and incompetent. He likened the GDR to a feudal state with paternalistic lords who amused themselves on hunting preserves. Conversely, he noted that the Politburo's hunting preserve did not have particularly large houses on it and that its small castle was used for meetings with diplomats and foreign politicians. Michael described the Stasi as a little army which had acquired much intelligence on the mood of the GDR masses, but whose reports were ignored by the SED elites. He said the Stasi agents could be easily identified because many of them dressed like West German insurance men with their tailored suits, chic leather jackets and custom hair-cuts.

Michael said that many of the party groups in the universities were reform-oriented, but suspected that the political atmosphere in factory party groups was probably much more restrictive. Although SED membership was a normal step in one's career, many university students had to wait a few years before being able to join the SED in order to ensure that a sufficient number of positions were available for workers. One needed two sponsors to be nominated for the SED. Following a probationary period of one year, a second vote was taken for full membership. Michael believed that SED members had to work harder than other GDR citizens. While many rank-and-file SED members were well aware of serious pollution problems in the GDR, few were willing to publicly speak out against them. Michael maintained in the two or three years prior to the Wende, many rank-and-file SED members had come to the realization that the party elites had lost control of the country. He said that members of the Academy of Science frequently had internal discussions about the economic and ideological crises of the GDR. Unfortunately, the SED had lost a sense of reality and tried to maintain an illusion of power.

Hannah's Story

Prior to 1991, Hannah worked as a university language instructor. She is divorced and presently lives with her boy friend and two sons in a relatively spacious apartment in Prenzlauer Berg that she renovated after the unification. Hannah's father had been a KPD member and later a SED member, and her mother had been a SPD member and later a SED member. In addition to being the technical director of a Fachhochschule (technical college), he was its SED secretary. Despite his relatively high position, he opposed many SED policies and criticized the personality cults centered around Walter Ulbricht and Erich Honecker. Hannah's father opposed the Soviet invasion of Czechoslovakia in 1968 in his party meetings. She said that her mother always agreed on political matters with her father. Hannah said that because she was more dogmatic on political matters at one time than now, she often had heated arguments with her father who encouraged open political discussions at home.

After completion of her university studies in French and English, Hannah obtained employment in 1975 as an interpreter at the foreign ministry where she met her former husband, Georg. In contrast to positions at Intertext, the GDR's interpretation agency, employment at the foreign ministry was considered to be a privilege because it entailed opportunities for travel, including to the West. Although she hated the hierarchy and regimentation of the ministry, Hannah came to enjoy her status as an inside-outsider. She made brief job-related trips to France and Switzerland. While she found both countries attractive, she had no desire to live in them but questioned why other GDR citizens could not travel to them as well. Hannah is not sure exactly why she joined the SED in 1977 other than perhaps to carry out her parents' mission. She describes herself as having been an ordinary rank-and-file party member. When Hannah's supervisor learned of her first pregnancy in 1979, he transferred her to the ministry's UNESCO commission where she worked primarily on translating documents. Because of her disenchantment with her work at the commission, she took a position in 1984 as an interpreter for a farm machinery export firm. Two years later Hannah became a university language instructor.

Although her former husband initially was a hard liner like herself, he became a critical thinker as a result of his doctoral studies at the Academy of Social Sciences. Despite its official affiliation with the ZK, the Academy functioned as an "oppositional institution" or a safety valve for intellectuals who by and large engaged in in-house critiques of GDR society which were used by the ZK as a source of information for better controlling the GDR masses. Hannah said that as a result of Georg's studies, the two of them began to develop "dream castles" on how the GDR could be transformed into an authentically democratic socialist society. While employed at the foreign ministry, she and Georg protested its restrictive environment by engaging in minor violations of diplomatic protocol, such as wearing jeans on a ministry boat ride.

Hannah said that party group discussions at both the foreign ministry and the export firm were very restricted. She said that two ministry staff involved in an extra-marital affair with each other were disciplined for their actions. Conversely, discussions in party group meeting at the university were quite open. Her party group decided to post its complaints to the *Kreisleitung* (circle leadership) on the bulletin board, but these were systematically ignored by the latter.

Thomas's Story

In 1991 Thomas served as the assistant director of a language school for foreign children and was a SED member prior to the Wende. He and his wife live with their daughter and son in an Altbau apartment in Pankow. His wife is also a school teacher, but never belonged to the SED. In September 1988, Thomas expressed his enthusiasm for Gorbachev's policies to me and criticized the privileges of the SED elites. On another occasion, while visiting him and his family in their Gartenhaus near Wandlitz, he drove me by the compound of the Politburo and also showed me a recreational area used by Honecker and other SED elites. He noted that many people from the provinces of the GDR despised East Berliners because resources, such as on the occasion of the 750th anniversary of Berlin, had been diverted to make East Berlin the showcase of the GDR.

Thomas stated that many SED members were critical of the GDR state and that a sharp distinction existed between the views of party elites and those of rank-and-file members. He said that many SED members sought greater intellectual openness within the party and the state. Thomas felt that *Neue Zeit*, a magazine published in the Soviet Union, was once considered boring reading but had become to be regarded by intellectuals as the most exciting periodical available in the GDR. He also asserted that *Junge Welt* (*Young World*), the FDJ magazine, was also interesting, in part because it was not directly controlled by the SED. Thomas said that many of the statistics in the GDR's yearbook had been manipulated and that many East Germans didn't consider the claims of the SED leadership on the economic achievements of the GDR to be reliable. He said that no one knows how many people worked for or collaborated with Stasi, although he estimated that perhaps between one in ten to twenty East Germans did.

Dieter's Story

Until he was expelled from the SED in 1979 for his unorthodox interpretations of Marxism-Leninism, Dieter was a philosophy lecturer at Humboldt University. While still a student, he was also expelled from the SED in 1958 for protesting the expulsion of Professor Ernst Bloch from the University of Leipzig. Although having vacillated in his obedience to the party line, Bloch was an inspiring teacher who was revered by his students. He argued that utopian endeavors often underwent a process of stagnation in which they became concerned with "pacification, order, and symmetry" (Bronner 1994:63). At any rate, Dieter obtained a job as a switchman at the Hauptbahnhof (main train station) in Leipzig - a position that he humbly accepted since he regarded himself as a member of the working class. He described his father as a "real worker" who had many economic problems until after World War II after which he became a master worker and a department head. After working as a switchman for three years, Dieter was admitted as a medical student at Humboldt University. Shortly thereafter, however, he switched his field of study back to philosophy. He was readmitted into the SED in 1963 after apologizing for his earlier "errors." Although he did not really believe that he had done anything wrong in the first place, he justified his recantation by telling himself that the SED leaders were ignorant and that he could accomplish more good by working within the SED rather than outside of it. After finishing his dissertation and obtaining his doctor of philosophy degree, Dieter was promoted to the position of Assistant and later *Oberassistant* (upper assistant). He felt that he was successful in his endeavors to teach students about classical Marxist writings.

Although he differed on various points with the orthodox Marxist theory of the SED, this did not create problems for him in his university teaching position. However, the lectures, such as those that he gave at a GDR-USSR joint corporation in Wismar and to physicians, and the papers that he presented outside of the university offended certain SED leaders. Dieter taught that a classless society would only be possible after the full development of capitalism and that Lenin had asserted that a successful socialist-oriented revolution in Russia ultimately depended upon the success of the German revolution. Dieter also argued that socialism is impossible without democracy. As much as he despised the anti-democratic policies of the SED leadership, he believed that this was a necessary stage for the ultimate achievement of socialism in the GDR. Dieter appealed his expulsion before the Control Commission (a body consisting of 15 to 20 social scientists and SED functionaries). After a long presentation of his views, the commission ruled that he deviated from the party's official theory on ten points.

As a result of his expulsion from the SED in 1979, he was forbidden from teaching and from pursuing research for a dissertation (which would have led to a doctor of science degree). Later he was ordered to stop allowing students to visit him in his apartment. Dieter was given a position at the university translating Marxist texts from English and Russian to German. In the process of deciphering some of Marx's handwriting - a mixture of German and English, Dieter witnessed first-hand the intellectual insights and shortcoming of this great figure. He felt that the SED leadership was not interested in theory, but rather wanted to maintain the status quo. Dieter maintained that the SED became a victim of its own propaganda, which it promulgated in order to ensure the smooth operation of GDR society. SED elites retreated into an encapsulated world in which their privileges took on a counterrevolutionary character. Dieter also maintained that the intelligentsia as a stratum of the working class increasingly became estranged from the working class. Workers became the most alienated stratum in GDR society and retreated into a culture of consumption. Dieter felt that the image of the GDR workers as lazy was a distorted stereotype. While some workers indeed took many breaks as a subtle form of protest against the GDR state, most of them were eager to work effectively but were forced to take long breaks as a result of late deliveries. Dieter said that while many rank-and-file SED members were committed socialists who had open discussions in their party groups, many academics felt forced to compartmentalize their private views and their public presentations. He believed that the poverty of Third World peoples will eventually act as a force of global revolution.

The SED From Below

In this chapter, I have examined the views and experiences of several former individuals who were either rank-and-file SED or held minor positions of leadership within the party. They were not typical SED members but neither were they atypical. While the SED had more than its share of hard liners, many of its members, like Walter, Petra, and others with whom I became acquainted, recognized the flaws of the GDR state, but tried to further the development of socialism in the best way that they knew how under extremely difficult circumstances. Many rank-and-file SED members argued that the GDR had to undergo a process of economic and political democratization before it achieved socialism.

Robert Havemann (1972), a former SED member and an eminent chemist at Humboldt University, asserted that the continuation of a neo-Stalinist dictatorship prevented the development of a democratic and ecologically sensitive socialism in the GDR. His heretical views resulted in expulsion from the SED, dismissal from his teaching position, and in house arrest. Rudolf Bahro (1978), a former SED member and an economist, called for a democratized party, termed the "League of Communists" and both social needs and the natural environment. Some former SED members were involved in the peace and environmental movements in the GDR and helped organize alternative political groups, such as New Forum and United Left which continue to function as part of the new opposition in East Germany. Others, as we will see in Chapter

7, become involved in the PDS, the reconstituted SED, which functions as part of the new opposition in the new German states.

Chapter 5

East Germany Revisited: The Aftermath of the Unification

The East Germany that I saw between 31 January and 7 April 1991 and again briefly in July 1991 was a very different place than the GDR that I had witnessed during 1988-1989 and that I had read and seen reports about on television during the euphoric days of the Wende. East Germany was still and continues to be a place filled with contradictions and tragedy. On the positive side, East Germans no longer needed to fear the surveillance of the Stasi. If they had the financial resources, they now had access to the material goods that the capitalist culture of consumption provides. On the negative side, the majority of East Germans faced an enormous amount of insecurity as the realities of the political merger of the two Germanies affected them on a daily basis and in a multiplicity of ways. Most East Germans assumed that their rich brothers and sisters in West Germany would help them achieve the good life associated with the *soziale Marktwirkschaft* (social market economy) of the FRG. As the *Treuhandanstalt* (the government agency that privatized former GDR state firms and properties) closed down numerous economic enterprises, many East Germans found themselves unemployed or facing the prospect of being unemployed in the near future. The Treuhand was created in early March 1990 by the GDR state in order to privatize the state combines. According to the new FRG laws, the state combines were required to reincorporate as AGs (public limited companies) by the end of 1990. The Treuhand was expected to function as more than a "holding company for eastern German industry but, rather, an agency that would transfer most of the companies in private (and not just German hands)" (Haendel 1991:105).

Out of a labor force of just under a million, *Neues Deutschland* (the former SED newspaper) reported the statistics illustrated in Table 3 below on the East German job market on February 7, 1991:

Table 3.
Unemployment in East Germany,
1990-1991

	Unemployed	Part-Time Work
July 1990	272,000	656,000
January 1991	757,200	1,855,500

The designation *Kurzarbeiter* ("part-time worker") refers to workers who are employed on a part-time basis or have been retained by a firm on its work force but do not work at all. One report stated: "By the end of 1991, according to some estimates, more than half of all eastern Germans will be unemployed and only 20 percent of the businesses from the old Communist regime will be operating" (*U.S. News & World Report*, April 1, 1991, p. 48).

Even those East Germans who were able to retain their jobs found that their wages (about 40 percent on the whole at the time of their West German counterparts) were inadequate to pay for the rising living costs, including those for utilities, public transportation, and recreation. East Germans faced massive rental increases and other price boosts as well as cuts in social services.

Criminality had become a major social problem in East Germany and many East Germans feared venturing outside of their homes at night. Gangs of alienated working-class youth (often referred to as "skinheads" or *Fachos*) adopted Nazi slogans and symbols and terrorized foreign workers, especially those from Vietnam and Africa, as scapegoats for the economic hardships of the new German states.

The Sights and Sounds of the Unification

My revisit occurred shortly after the formal unification of the two Germanies on 3 October 1990. As the Frankfurt-Berlin express passed between Bebra and Gerlungen, I could see the posts of the former Iron Curtain. Other than the remnants of the Iron Curtain, my first hint that the unification was only in its initial stages was when the conductors of the *Deutschebahn* (the FRG's national rail system) replaced those of the *Reichsbahn* (the former GDR's national rail system) at Gerlungen. As the train passed between Bahnhof Zoo in West Berlin and Bahnhof Friedrichstrasse in East Berlin, I could see the remnants of the infamous Berlin Wall. My first direct hint that prices had increased in East Germany since the unification was that, in contrast to my earlier stay, I had to pay two D-Marks instead of one Ostmark to store my luggage at the train station and thirty *Pfenning* instead of ten Pfenning to call my friend and colleague, Walter Rusch, at whose apartment at Kastienalle 74 in Prenzlauer Berg, an old working-class district with a strong bohemian flavor, I would be staying for the next two months. Since the Wall in the vicinity in Bernauer Strasse was now dismantled, I could easily walk in five minutes to West Berlin.

Part of the Wall along Bernauer Strasse had been designated as a *Gedenkstaette* (memorial). Crosses at various points along the former Wall marked the places where people had been killed trying to escape to the West. Walter confessed that he still became disoriented when he walked in this section of West Berlin, even though it was a very short distance from his apartment. Like many East Berliners, he carried a map with him when visiting West Berlin because the landmarks and streets were so new to him, despite the fact that he had visited that part of the divided city before the erection of the Wall in 1961. Kaisers, a West German grocery chain, had bought up the state-operated Kaufhalle in Walter's neighborhood. During the winter of 1991, Kaisers, like the other West German chains that had purchased the GDR-state grocery stores, sold no or very few East German products. They even imported fresh dairy and meat products and bakery goods into East Berlin and other East German cities and towns from far-off locations in West Germany. This practice, needless to say, contributed heavily to the collapse of the East German food production industry. Eberswalder, an East German firm, was forced to sell its meat products on the street and in the vicinity of the *U-Bahn* (subway) and *S-Bahn* (rapid transit train) stations. Conversely, stories abounded that at least for a period of time many East Germans preferred to buy West German staples merely because they had been produced in West Germany, even if the quality of the East German products was on the same level. The shop windows throughout East Germany displayed almost exclusively West German products.

Since many East Germans had used their life savings after the currency exchange to purchase Western automobiles (often used ones), East Berlin and other East German cities were now experiencing unprecedented traffic problems and an increase in auto accidents and fatalities. According to Merkl (1993:298), "East Germans reportedly have bought up every used car on the West German lots and quite a few new cars as well, easily 2 million vehicles in 1990/91." Indeed, in 1991 my cousin, Georg, became the proud owner of a new car that he purchased in the medium-sized city of Celle in Lower Saxony. Crossing Unter den Linden had become much more of a dodge-'em endeavor than in the past. Throughout East Germany, one could see the shells of discarded and stripped two-cylinder Trabants. Many East Germans also purchased new color television sets, video recorders, stereo systems, furniture, carpeting, clothing, and just about every conceivable product offered by the capitalist culture of consumption. Because prices were generally lower in West Berlin than in East Berlin, many East Berliners and other East Germans made regular shopping forays to West Berlin and towns and cities near the former GDR-FRG border, much to the annoyance of their West German brothers and sisters.

I often had the sense that East Germany had been transformed into a quasi-nation of vendors as seemingly everywhere one saw open-air markets selling all manner of cheap wares from capitalist countries as well as staple foods, such as vegetables, fruit, bakery products. Kiosks and open newsstands carried a wide assortment of West German newspapers, including *Das Bild* (the Springer right-wing, scandal tabloid so popular among a large segment of the German working class), and magazines, including pornographic ones that were prohibited in the GDR. New publications, such as *Super Illu* and *Extra Maqazine*, specialized in reporting on scandals that occurred both within the SED regime, particularly the Stasi, as well as the economic hardships of East Germans in the new Germany. A variety of alternative periodicals, such as *Die Andere: Unabhaenigie Wochenzeitung fuer Politik, Kultur u. Kunst (The Alternative: An Independent Weekly on Politics, Culture and Art), Berliner Linke (Berliner Leftist),* and *Die Leipziger Andere Zeitung (The Leipzig Alternative Newspaper)* catered to those who eschewed the more popular scandal tabloids.

Young Vietnamese men and women, who originally were brought to the GDR as apprentices but in time came to function along with Angolans, Mozambicans, Ethiopians, and Cubans as GDR guest workers sold cigarettes in American name brand cartons on the street or at the entrance of transit stations. Alexanderplatz, particularly in the vicinity of the S-Bahn and U-Bahn stations, became transformed into a colorful and hectic collection of such enterprises, many of which were operated by Turks from West Berlin. In the same vicinity, one saw young Polish men conducting a gambling game in which on-lookers placed bets of 100 Marks as they tried to figure out under which of three match boxes the performers placed a little white ball before quickly shuffling them around. If one was lucky enough to guess under which box the performer had placed the ball or even had managed to follow the rapid movement of his hands, he (It always seemed to be a "he") would receive a two-to-one pay-off. The willingness of some East Germans to depart with their short supply of D-Marks always amazed me, even though I was well aware of the lure of "lady-luck" for the down-and-out in many cultures. I never once saw the police attempt to break up these games. Occasionally the passer-by might be accosted by a member of the Hare Krishna sect, which had been banned in the GDR, trying to provide one with their sacred text for a donation.

Many East Germans had attempted to become entrepreneurs by establishing a wide variety of small businesses, including fast food restaurants, Imbiss (snack) stands, beauty and sauna parlors, and video-shops (which found themselves in stiff competition with West German video chains). Some East Germans operated such establishments inside their homes. On Kollwitz Strasse in Prenzlauer Berg, a physician advertised his new practice featuring acupuncture, neural therapy, reflex zone therapy, yoga, and other alternative therapies which were virtually unknown in the GDR. In Cranzahl, a village in the Erzgebirge, I visited Cafe Rose which was established in July 1990. The petit bourgeois ambience of its two eating rooms -- one of them in pink decor and the other in Germanic medieval decor -- seemed completely out of character with Cranzahl's rather shabby appearance. Perhaps the proprietor of the cafe had hoped for a flood of affluent Western German tourists to find their way to his establishment as they drove through the area. West German insurance agents routinely rang doorbells seeking to sell policies of all sorts to their East German brothers and sisters.

On one occasion, a teenage girl rang Walter's doorbell and presented him with a candle and candle-holder set as a gift for listening to her spiel about her new business. She was taking orders for various West German newspapers that she would personally deliver. The young entrepreneur explained that she could not find an apprenticeship (something which she would have obtained upon completion of Oberschule in the GDR) and had no hope of finding a good job in the new Germany for the foreseeable future. As a consequence, she had taken on this job in order to earn a *Groschen* (small coin or penny). She explained that while she received four Marks for each subscription that she managed to sell, she felt lucky when she sold one in an hour's time. In contrast to my stay in the GDR, I also witnessed a number of beggars in East Berlin during the winter of 1991.

As opposed to the abundance of new consumer items, I repeatedly saw evidence that East Germans were not eating out, visiting their favorite pubs or cafes, or attending movies and the theater nearly as often as they did in the past due to large increases in prices for these amenities. Many restaurants were virtually deserted, including on Friday and Saturday evenings when it was generally difficult to obtain a table during GDR days. The proletarian restaurant beneath the Fernsehnturm had far fewer customers when I dropped in on 4 February 1991 than I ever remember it having in the past.

Certain fashionable East Berlin nightspots (such as the cafe on the top of the French Cathedral (*Franzoische Dom*), however, had become very popular with West Berliners. Whereas the 7:30 pm showing of Volker Braun's *Europa Transit* at the popular Maxim Gorki Theater played to a house only a quarter filled on February 9, 1991, such a performance would have been sold-out prior to the Wende. Tickets for the performance ranged in price from 28 Marks to 6 Marks. Although a comedy titled *Du bist dran, ich pass* ("You are on, I pass") played to a near full house on the evening of 4 March 1991, most of those in the audience appeared to be West Berliners, many of whom had probably discovered that plays are still cheaper, although much less so, than in the past, in East Berlin than in West Berlin. When I attended the 7:30 pm showing of *Der Tango Spieler* ("The Tango Player") -- an excellent East German film -- on Friday, 1 March 1991, I counted some 35-40 people in the large auditorium of *Kino International* on *Karl Marx Alle*. Needless to say, such a showing would have been sold-out prior to the Wende as well.

As I wandered around East Berlin and other parts of East Germany over the next couple of months, I saw numerous symbols of the Wende and the unification. The insignia of the GDR state consisting of a hammer and a compass had been removed from the *Palast der Republic* (Palace of the Republic). This multi-purpose building, which once housed the Volkskammer had been closed, "ostensibly because asbestos was used in parts of construction, even though the readings on asbestos in the air are well within otherwise permissible levels" (Marcuse 1991:282). The presence of asbestos prompted some politicians to argue that it should be torn down because renovation costs would be excessive. Many East Germans interpreted this proposal as one more example of West German colonization (*Kolonisierung*). There were even rumors that the *Fernsehturm* (television tower) in Alexanderplatz would be torn down. The German Historical Museum, whose exhibits the SED regime had organized according to Marx's historical periods, had been closed for renovations until September 1991. Nevertheless, as late as my visit in July of 1991, many symbols of the GDR state remained -- including in East Berlin the statue of Marx and Engels in Marx-Engels Platz, the large statue of Lenin, and street names such as Karl Marx Alle, Otto Grotewohl Strasse, and Ho Chi Minh Strasse. The eventual dismantling of the statue of Lenin several months later prompted a protest demonstration.

Vans chauffeured tourists from Unter den Linden to the former compound of the Politburo in Wandlitz along the former protocol stretch along which Erich Honecker and members of the Politburo were chauffeured in a motorcade to their offices in East Berlin. While larger than most East German houses, Erich Honecker's former drab-gray stucco residence at the settlement is certainly unimpressive by Western standards for a head-of-state. Nevertheless, East Germans were outraged when they learned details about the amenities, including access to many Western goods, that SED elites enjoyed.

Left-over election posters proclaimed the campaign promises of the various new political parties for the future of the new German states. Posters for the coalition of the Christian Democratic Union and the German Social Union (*Deutsche Sociale Union*) included statements such as "*Wir helfen den Opern von SED u. Stasi*" ("We help the victims of the SED and the Stasi") and "*Nie wieder Sozialismus. Freibeit u. Wohlstand*" ("Never again socialism. Freedom and prosperity"). A poster for the coalition of the Alliance 90 and the Greens stated: "*Mehr Farben bracht das Land*" ("The country needs more colors"). As opposed to East Berlin where I saw many PDS and Buendnis and few DSU/CDU posters, I saw many CDU and DSU/CSU (Christian Social Union - the Bavarian sister party of the CDU) posters in southern East German cities such as Chemnitz (Karl Marx Stadt in the GDR), Dresden, Meissen, and Annaberg-Buchholz (a small city in the Erzgebirge) and none for PDS and only one for Alliance 90.

Commercial establishments even posted placards and stickers celebrating the unification. For example, the Berliner Bank and Stadtbank distributed a bumper sticker stating, "*Hurra, jetzt stepp der Baer in ganz Berlin*" ("Hurrah, now the bear [the mascot of the city of Berlin] walks in all of Berlin"). Advertisements introduced new expressions into the East German language such as *Risiko* (risk) and *Sonderpreis* (special price) and a wide variety of English expressions which are common in West Germany. Graffiti demanded that amnesty not be given to Stasi agents and collaborators and one piece of graffiti that I saw near Alexanderplatz read, "*Gorbaschow ist ein roter Faschist*" ("Gorbachev is a red fascist").

Perhaps the most amusing symbol of the unification that I experienced was a West German film titled "Go, Trabi. Go'" which made a big hit in East Germany. Indeed, as Borneman (1992:55) observes, the Trabant itself served as a symbol of East German identity which embodied images of a petty bourgeois people with an inferiority complex who were confined to a state-dominated homeland. At any rate, the film delightfully portrays the misadventures of an East German literature teacher who with his wife and teenage daughter embarks upon a summer auto journey in the family's beloved Trabant from Bitterfeld, one of the most polluted cities in East Germany, to Naples by following the route of Goethe's famous journey. The family's first visit is with their obese Bavarian relatives consisting of a married couple and their gluttonous teenage son. Along the way, the family's Trabi has its tires stolen and the teacher's wife and daughter have romantic escapades while he tries to keep the Trabi in operating condition. In order to meet expenses incurred by the family auto, at one point in the trip they sell rides around a town square in their Trabi. Following many trials and tribulations, the tiny Trabi manages to deliver its East German owners to the outskirts of Naples as it careens over a cliff into the sea below, ending its fulfilled life now that it has seen Naples.

A grimmer symbol of the political merger of the two Germanies were signs of protest against the new rulers. Demonstrations against the Treuhand by workers were regularly reported in the newspapers and on television. An estimated 80,000 people in Leipzig demonstrated on a Monday night on 12 March 1991 (Merkl 1993:288). The various demonstrations were organized by trade unions, citizens and church groups, pacifists, and the SPD and PDS. I myself witnessed a demonstration of some 300-400 metalworkers in front of the Treuhandanstalt at 6 Alexander Strasse across from Alexanderplatz on 14 March 1991. A flyer distributed by the metalworkers' union read: "We further the reconstruction of companies -- the insurance of jobs instead of the destruction of jobs through privatization. Unionists of all federal states, unite!!!" In addition to East Berlin and Leipzig, *Demos* occurred in many other East German cities.

In March 1991 Alliance 90 organized Monday demonstrations (a new tradition during the Wende) which were also attended by representatives from PDS, SPD, and the Spartakists (a Trotskyist group) in Leipzig, Berlin, and other East German cities. On 4 April 1991, Detlev Rohwedder, the Treuhand head, was assassinated in his home in Duesseldorf. The *Rote Arme Fraktion* (the Red Army Group), a Western German ultra-leftist organization, claimed responsibility for the killing, but it was rumored that the ex-Stasis were behind the act, apparently because the Stasi and the Rote Arme had once collaborated with each other. Demonstrations against the Gulf War were also commonplace in East Germany in early 1991. The *Jugend Verein* (Youth Association) in coalition with Peace Team, a British group, erected a *Gedenkenwerkstatt* (reflection workshop) in front of the Monument Against Fascism on Unter den Linden. A small group of students camped in front of the main building at Humboldt University as a permanent vigil against the war. A small sign on a box containing used books for sale read: "*Links tut gut. Wir bleiben das Volk.*" ("Left is good. We remain the people"). Demonstrators marched daily to Alexanderplatz to protest the war, and a week-long *Friedenskamp* (peace camp) occurred at the Brandenburg Gate in early February 1991. Opposition groups, including Alliance 90, United Left, the *Kommunistische Platform in der PDS* (Communist Platform in PDS), and the *Gruppe Revoluntaere Sozialist Innen* (Revolutionary Socialist Group from Within), regularly conducted talks and panel discussions in opposition to the war. Peace vigils occurred regularly at many churches throughout East Germany. In anticipation of possible protests, policemen guarded the barricaded premises of the former American Embassy in East Berlin during the course of the war. Squatter settlements occupied by young anarchists and punks displayed banners opposing the Gulf War and imperialism. Many of these apartments had a GDR flag draped outside of them, probably more as a protest against the unification than as a celebration of the former GDR.

On 14 March 1991, I attended a talk by Regine Hildebrandt, the SPD Minister of Labor of the new state of Brandenburg at the Evangelical church in Heinersdorf, an area in the northern section of East Berlin. She told the audience that the unemployment rate in Brandenburg stood at 25-30 percent. When she was invited to speak at a forthcoming Monday demonstration in Cottbus, Hildebrandt asked the SPD Minister-President of Brandenburg if she should accept the invitation, which he said that she should. She encouraged church people to become more politically active, including on economic issues, and urged those in the audience to participate in the Monday demonstrations that had started up again in East Germany. The Minister of Labor noted that she is a Berliner and favors the creation of Berlin-Brandenburg as a new German state.

Travels in East Germany with a Group of Ami Academics

In July 1991 I had another opportunity to visit East Germany as one of twenty-two participants in a Fulbright Kommission seminar in German studies which focused on the German unification. The seminar took place during the period of 22 June - 24 July in various locations in the new Germany. The lectures and talks by professors, government bureaucrats, and military officers in Bonn and Kiel during the period of 22 June 22 - 8 July provided us with a Western German perspective on the unification. While some of the speakers admitted that the GDR social system had some redeeming features, the thrust of their comments either explicitly stated or implied that East Germans would by-and-large have to make unilateral adjustments to the FRG political economy. At times I had the sense that the speakers were comparing the worst of the GDR system with a sentimental model of the FRG. I quickly found myself in the uncomfortable role of protagonist by challenging periodically the GDR-bashing character of many of the presentations. I repeatedly reiterated that while I did not wish to defend the atrocities of the SED regime, I felt that it was important to recognize the GDR had at least some significant positive features.

Fortunately, the seminar did permit the participants to obtain a somewhat more balanced view of the unification process by providing the opportunity to visit East Germany during the period of 9 - 24 July. In the remainder of this section, I present a day-by-day account of my travels with a group of Amis, eight of whom were actually born in Germany, through East Germany.

9 July 1991

Our chartered bus crossed the former GDR-FRG border on the east side of the famous Hanseatic city of Luebeck and carried us through the Mecklenberg countryside and made stops in Wismar, Bad Doberan, Heiligendamm (a famous spa or *Kurort* on the Baltic Sea) on our way to Rostock. Given that most of the seminar participants had never been to East Germany, I wanted to obtain their initial impressions to what they were seeing.

One participant said that what he saw outside of the bus window did not strike him as bad as what he had been led to believe would be the case in Bonn. He noted that the East German village of Selmsdorf looked better than many small towns in his home state of Iowa. The participants, however, found the city center of Wismar, East Germany's second largest seaport, in bad shape. A female participant, who had received the impression in Bonn of a collapsed East German infrastructure, said that many of the cities and towns in western Pennsylvania -- the area where she was reared -- look worse than those that she had seen that day in Mecklenberg. Another participant said that based on what he had heard in Bonn, he had expected to see East Germans living in chicken coops. A second female participant felt that the towns and villages in northern France are in a more dilapidated state than those in Mecklenberg and stated that the presentations in Bonn focused more on the negative living conditions in the East German cities than in the villages and countryside. Conversely, a third female participant asked how people could have believed in social system that provided such a poor standard of living. After touring the center of Rostock, two participants noted that its city center looked "pretty good."

In Wismar a city planner provided the seminar group with a guided walking tour of the city center. He spoke of proposals to construct an underground parking garage below the *Marktplatz* (marketplace) and to develop a 250 meter walking zone around the Marketplatz and a system of mini-buses that that would transport people to it. The city planner noted that while the city planning commission does not wish to transform the *Zentrum* (city center) into a museum, it wants to avoid the mistakes that many West German cities made after World War II when their centers became converted into primarily commercial areas. The St. Georgenkirche (St. George's Church) is undergoing reconstruction with financial support from the *Deutschen Stiftung Denkmalschutz* (German Foundation for Protection of Monuments). The city planner also noted that Wismar would receive natural gas lines within the next year and a half, a development that would begin to counteract the environmental damage from the brown coal or lignite heating systems that the GDR relied so heavily upon.

In addition to discussing the positive developments that unification would bring to the infrastructure of Wismar, the city planner discussed in some detail the social problems that it has created and may create in the future for people of the city and the region. As he showed the group a music school that had been established in 1949 on the site of what had been Mecklenberg's first engineering school, he noted that the future of the school was uncertain because students may not be able to pay its tuition fees. The city planner expressed concern that Mecklenberg-Vorpommern might revert back to its former status as a backwater area in Germany. He lamented that many West Germans assert that East Germans are not thankful enough for West German assistance. In turn, the East Germans counter that they kept the Russians away from West Germany. The city planner said that the Wende was not a revolution but a collapse of a social system and that East Germans were disappointed with the unification process because the FRG is attempting to force East Germany into its model. He joked: "If we have too many problems, we will join Sweden. The Danes and Swedes speak more gently with us than do the West Germans."

10 July

Our seminar group met in the morning with government bureaucrats in Rostock's *Rathaus* (city hall). We were told that Rostock's shipbuilding industry was in a serious state of decline due to a lack of orders from the Soviet Union and would have to undergo renovation. One speaker noted that East Germany is being overrun by West German sales operations which extract capital from the region, adding that tourism would not be sufficient to support the local economy. A female representative from the *Umwelt Amt* (environmental office) observed that the city has been unsuccessful in its efforts to have West German distributors sell beverages in returnable containers rather than throw-away ones. She lamented that the recycling system of the GDR, in which children gathered used paper, bottles, and bottle caps, broke down after the Wende. A representative from the city planning commission noted that while planning has negative connotations under the new system, some planning is necessary. He added that while the GDR had good environmental policies, the state did not adequately enforce them. Our third speaker noted that Rostock cannot be supported solely from the operations of small companies and that wages in East Germany must be raised significantly to deter its people from immigrating to West Germany. He said that East Germans keep on discovering that large West German companies are moving into the economic niches which the former had hoped to fill as small business people. Indeed, a large floating West German-owned shopping center called the Plaza is now docked on the Warnow River in Rostock. Furthermore, many East Germans have difficulty obtaining credit to start new businesses. Another speaker asserted that Schwerin was chosen as the new capital of Mecklenberg-Vorpommern rather than Rostock because the latter has a reputation as a former SED power center in the region.

11 July

Our seminar group had a meeting with officials from various ministries in the *Staatskanzlei* (chancery office) in Schwerin (pop. 139,492) -- the capital of the new German state of Mecklenberg-Vorpommern and the former home of the dukes of Mecklenberg. Since the *Land* (state) elections of 14 October 1990, the Christian Democrats had governed in coalition with the Free Democrats. The coalition, however, held a slender voting edge over the opposition consisting of the SPD and PDS. One of the speakers noted that antagonism toward foreigners in Mecklenberg-Vorpommern had been directed more toward Africans and the Vietnamese, most of whom had lost their jobs after the Wende, than Poles since the former had been invited to East Germany by the GDR state. A representative of the Department of Higher Education in the Ministry of Culture told us that Mecklenberg-Vorpommern has an excessive number of faculty and staff at its six institutions of higher education (Rostock University, Greifswald University, two teachers colleges, a college of technology, and a college of navigation). She noted that Rostock University alone has some 4,900 employees, but the number of employees for all six institutions would have to be trimmed to 4,000. According to the representative, moral guilt rather than rank-and-file SED membership would be one of the criteria for dismissal. A physician said that the GDR state exhibited a mixed record on public health issues. Although it banned cigarette advertisements and machines, it failed to publish statistics on suicide rates. Recycling of plastic containers was easier before the Wende than now because the GDR produced a smaller number and variety of plastic containers than does the FRG. The physician also noted that despite the existence of environmental protection laws in the GDR, economic considerations overrode their enforcement.

12 July

Our seminar group visited Greifswald University (est. 1556), one of the ten oldest universities in what once was the Holy Roman Empire. The *Prorektor* stated that the university plans to develop connections with Swedish and Polish universities and to become a center of Scandinavian and Baltic language studies. He noted that many of the some 280 faculty members (who serve some 3,300 students) and 1,800 researchers (many of whom are affiliated with the medical school) will be dismissed due to lack of funds.

In a meeting at Greifswald's Rathaus, the mayor, a pastor who was politically active during the Wende, said that the term *Vorpommern* (West Pomerania) emerged as a result of local "patriotism" during the Wende. He said that Greifswald (pop. 68,270) needs the reconstruction of a major railroad line that would connect it directly with Sweden in the north and Berlin, Dresden, Prague, and Budapest in the south if it is to overcome its backwater status. The mayor speculated that a projected expansion of the university to 9,000 students would also assist the city's economy. He noted that East Germans need a balance of the socialist ideal of justice and the Western ideal of freedom.

13 July

A waiter in the nightclub on the top floor of the Neptune Hotel overlooking the seaside resort of Warnemuende and the Baltic Sea (Ostsee) told several of the seminar participants that members of the Free German Trade Union Federation (FDGB) received a room in the hotel for 350 Ostmarks for ten days and that about 80 percent of the hotel's guests prior to the Wende were GDR citizens.

14 July

On our bus ride from Rostock to Berlin, one of the seminar participants told me that two female receptionists at the Hotel Warnow in Rostock told her that many East Germans now feel that they can't say anything positive about the former GDR. Whereas they had the freedom to complain to their Chef about working conditions under the GDR system, the receptionists asserted that they now fear loosing their jobs if they would engage in such behavior under the new system.

15 July

The seminar group met with several speakers in the conference room of a building that once housed the Ministry of Higher Education of the GDR. An attractive wooden map showing the location of "DDR Hoch-und-Fachschulen" (GDR colleges, universities, and trade schools)

served as a reminder of the former occupants of the building. The state
secretary (a West Berliner) from the Administration for Science and
Research of the Berlin Senate spoke in detail about the allegedly poor
conditions of the GDR's educational system. She maintained that many
employees in GDR institutions of higher learning had little work to do, an
assertion which did not correspond with my observations during my
Fulbright Lectureship in the GDR. After eating lunch at the Restaurant
Schinkel-Klause (a favorite eating spot of Erich Honecker) on
Oberwallstrasse across the street from the building that once housed the
GDR's Council of Ministers, we heard a talk on "The German Unification
Process from the Church's Perspective" by Johannes Richter, D.D., the
pastor of the Thomaskirche in Leipzig. In asking the meaning of being a
Christian in the new Germany, he expressed concern about the impact of
the western material standard of living (in part by what he termed the
German love for the automobile) on religious values. Pastor Richter
observed that a sense of frustration now exists between the East German
and West German churches. For example, whereas the West German
church had urged the East German church to adopt the FRG's church tax
system and military draft, the East German church viewed the tax system
as problematic as a form of subsidization because of the low level of
church membership in the new German states. Richter also noted that the
Jugendweihe (the youth consecration ceremony) meant to compete with
Christian confirmation in the GDR, continues to survive in East Germany.

16 July

The seminar group met with various representatives from the city
parliament of Templin in the state of Brandenburg, which gave a plurality
to the SPD in the October 1990 elections. Brandenburg is governed by a
coalition led by SPD Premier Manfred Stolpe and including the Free
Democratic Party (FDP) and Alliance 90. The Buergermeister of Templin
is a member of the SPD and the city parliament consists of 10 SPD
representatives, 9 CDU representatives, 3 PDS representatives, 2 FDP
representatives, 1 Farmers' Party representative, and 2 non-party
representatives, one of whom belongs to the New Forum. One of the FDP
representatives, a teacher in his forties, told us that East Germans were
unprepared for the transition to a market economy because they are afraid
to seek credit and take risks. He noted that many East Germans left the
political parties because they became disillusioned with social conditions
in East Germany after the Wende, adding that he himself sometimes felt

like a second-class citizen, especially when West German civil servants earn more money in East Germany than East Germans do. The other FDP representative complained that many former SED managers continue to hold management positions in East German firms.

17 July

The seminar group met in round table talks with members of the Bezirk council of Koepenick in East Berlin. Koepenick is governed by a SPD/CDU coalition. The first speaker, a middle-aged man, argued that the changes in the Soviet Union and reductions in tensions between the super-powers had paved the way for the Wende and unification in East Germany and asserted that not everything in the GDR was bad. A middle-aged woman also noted that some things in the GDR functioned well. She commented upon the growing hostilities that had developed since unification between East Germans and West Germans, including even between family members. A middle-aged male representing Alliance 90 observed that unification is like a wedding in that both require a period of adjustment. He joked that now there are hardly any lines in East Germany, except at the banks. Another middle-aged man stated that "We must learn to adapt to a competitive system with a social net."

During the luncheon, a female physician representing Alliance 90 told the seminar participants at her table that the unification constitutes a West German colonization of East Germany -- an assertion that many West Germans detest. I sat at a table with a representative from Alliance 90/New Forum and a CDU representative. The NF representative, a civil engineer who wanted to start his own engineering firm, argued that the issue of Berlin as the new capital of Germany was more important for West Germans than East Germans. He complained that the first thing that many West German government bureaucrats want to do upon assuming administrative positions in East Germany is to renovate their offices. The CDU representative, a male instructor in a Volkshochschule (community college), noted that he favored the selection of Berlin as the new capital because it will become the locomotive that pulls united Germany.

In the afternoon, we heard a talk in which Manfred Rexin, a prominent West German media commentator, likened the West German East German confrontation during the unification process to the confrontation between the North and the South during Reconstruction following the American Civil War. Referring to long-term social divisions between the North and the South in the United States, he argued that West-East tensions will last at least a generation in Germany. While noting that many East Germans are better off as a result of the unification, he observed that hundreds and thousands of East Germans now face a worse socioeconomic situation. Rexin said that East Germans over the age of 50 in particular will have difficulty integrating into the new system. He argued the unification process has reinforced a sense of GDR identity among middle-aged and elderly East Germans and said that he is not sure how patient East Germans will be with the unification process in another two or three years. Rexin argued that West Germans need to recognize the positive features of GDR society. He observed that whereas the FRG has about 17,500 judges, the GDR had only some 1,200 judges. As a consequence, the FRG government has urged retired West German judges to serve for a few years in East Germany, an appeal that only a few hundred of them have accepted.

18 July

Our seminar group had round table discussions with several representatives (*Abgeordenten*) in the *Abgeordentenhaus von Berlin* in the Rathaus Schoenberg in West Berlin. A female representative from West Berlin representing *Buendnis 90/Gruene/Unhaenige Frauen Verband* - a coalition consisting of Alliance 90, the Greens, and the Independent Women's Association - maintained that a mood of resignation has developed in East Germany and that the political parties there were losing members. She pointed out that East Germany paid most of the reparations to World War II and asserted that West Germany could learn from the women's policies of the GDR state. A male FDP representative countered her position by arguing that the GDR state created certain social benefits for women as a strategy for incorporating them into the economy and for indoctrinating children. A CDU representative maintained that West Germany probably can learn little from the GDR social system, except perhaps something from the solidarity of its citizens in the face of adversity.

19 July

In a round table discussion on the status of foreigners in the new Germany, a civil servant attached to the Berlin Senate noted that many Germans feel that citizenship for foreigners should be contingent upon their willingness to assimilate into German culture, although she herself questioned a strict interpretation of this expectation. Instead she maintained that work is the primary ingredient for integration into German society.

21 July

I visited East Berlin friends at their Gartenhaus situated in a *Kleingartenanlage "Einigkeit"* (Small Garden Compound "Harmony") in Pankow/Niederschoenhausen/Rosenthal. The compound has some 8,000 parcels of land and some 10-12,000 members. About 80 percent of the land in the compound is city property. According to my friend Wolfgang, about 12 percent of the dwelling units in the compound are occupied year-round -- a practice that does not conform to FRG regulations. He noted that at one time the GDR state also discouraged people from residing year-round in garden house compounds because this practice reflected poorly upon socialism which in theory should have provided each family unit with adequate housing. Wolfgang maintained that the GDR state changed its policy in order to improve its housing statistics. He also stated that SED members were granted the best garden plots.

22 July

In the morning the seminar group met with a representative from the *Berliner Absatz-Organization* (BAO or Berlin Ready Sale Organization) and a representative from the *EG-Beratungsstelle* (Information Center of the European Community) in the *Industrieund Handleskammer zu Berlin* on Hardenbergstrasse. The representative noted that Berlin does not have much more room for internal commercial and industrial development but that the surrounding state of Brandenburg offers many such possibilities. He maintained that East Germans need to adapt (*anpassen*) to the new system. The EG representative spoke about the competition that has developed between the Free University and Humboldt University for positions and funding. She admitted that the GDR research efforts in biotechnology were at least on par with or perhaps even surpassed those of the FRG.

In the afternoon the seminar group met with a spokesperson of the *Deutsche Gewerkschaft Bund* (DGB or German Trade Union Association). He stated that the assassination of the head of the Treuhand in March contributed to a decline of protest demonstrations in East Germany and added that the unions chose not to participate in the Monday demonstrations that reappeared earlier in the year because they were more in the tradition of the Wende than that of trade union activism. The DGB spokesperson said that foreign workers are being laid off and being replaced by East Germans who are willing to accept lower wages.

Chapter 6

Reflections of East Germans on Life after the Wende

This chapter focuses on the observations shared with me by East Germans from various walks of life. The first part of the chapter focuses on the impact that the Wende and unification had on the lives of Walter and Petra whose experiences within the SED and the GDR were discussed in detail in Chapter 4. This is followed by a discussion of the experiences and perceptions of life in the new Germany of various other former SED members. The final section of this chapter discusses the experiences and perceptions that various East Germans who chose not to join the SED had of the changes that had occurred in East Germany after the unification.

The Lives of Walter and Petra after the Wende

Walter's Life in the New Germany

After the Wende, Walter became extremely depressed, even to the point of contemplating suicide. He felt that his work in the SED and the Liga had been without meaning. Furthermore, Bereich Ethnographie along with other programs and departments dealing with societal issues (namely history, law, sociology, philosophy, and education) initially were slated for *Abwicklung*, which meant that they would be dismantled and, except for the Department of Marxism-Leninism, would be reconstructed. After faculty members in these departments were laid off, the newly constructed departments would hire new faculty members as well as former faculty members deemed to be politically trustworthy. Walter was convinced that given his past leadership positions in the SED and the existence of many unemployed ethnologists in West Germany, his prospects of being rehired would be very slim.

In mid-1991, however, Professor Fink, the democratically-elected rector (president) of Humboldt University, won a court case in which he had challenged the constitutionality of the Abwicklung-a process of unwinding or unreeling-in the Land (state) of Berlin. As Borneman (1992:312) observes, the definitions of *Abwicklung* (noun) and *abwickeln* (verb) "capture two of the fundamental aspects of German unification: first, the GDR as a social formation, with its unique sets of practices and dispositions, will be unrolled and deconstructed to its thinnest, most unadorned and elementary units: second, this orderly and step-by-step unraveling is a final settling of Cold War accounts." At any rate, the Abwicklung policy was eventually upheld. In the interim while the status of the departments in question, except for the Department of Marxism-Leninism, remained pending, Walter was assigned to perform a number of housekeeping tasks in his department. Eventually all members of the ethnography department, including the sole full professor, were *abgewickelt* or lost their positions. Some faculty members found new positions before they could be officially terminated and others, including Walter, went into early retirement. Bereich Ethnographie, which included specialists on cultures outside of Europe, was reconstituted as the Institute of European Ethnology with a professor from the University of Tuebingen as its director and West Germans as new faculty members. Indeed, one of these new faculty members was trained in cultural sociology rather than in ethnography per se.

Walter eventually moved to Leipzig where his Saxon wife had found a position as the editor of the municipal newspaper with a mass circulation, after she had lost her job with a former GDR publishing firm. He has been working on various research projects and has held two visiting lectureships at Kampala University in Uganda.

Walter felt that East Germans were accomplices in the collapse. He himself felt guilty about having gone along with the abuses of power in the GDR. He felt that he was too old to struggle for socialist ideals. Walter resigned from the SED and did not choose to join the Party of Democratic Socialism, the reconstituted SED. He agreed with many of the ideas of various alternative political groups, such as the Greens, but felt that these groups were disorganized, unclear in their objectives, and marginal in German politics.

In 1991 Walter argued that the FRG had bought the GDR in a "clean sale." He complained that the grocery stores, which were bought up by FRG chains, stocked almost exclusively products out of West Germany.

Walter made a concerted effort to purchase East German products, many of which were sold outdoors and at subway and rapid transit stops. While he recognized that this was a minimal gesture, it symbolized his pride in the positive achievements of the GDR to which he dedicated his life, one which he painfully realized had been filled with contradiction.

Petra's Life in the New Germany

Whereas Walter was not fully aware of the extent to which the East German masses were dissatisfied with the GDR state, Petra's contacts with working-class friends provided her with insights that apparently many GDR intellectuals did not have. She said that when the masses shouted "Gorby! Gorby!" on the occasion of Gorbachev's visit to East Berlin in October 1989, they were really crying, "Help us! Help us!" For reasons which she could not explain, Petra could not get herself to visit West Berlin until three weeks after the Wall had been opened. As late as the summer of 1995, she confessed to me that she seldom had made forays into West Berlin, which felt like a foreign country to her. She said that the Wende was particularly traumatic for her parents, who were unaware of many of the contradictions of GDR society, perhaps because they had spent so much time as journalists in the West. Petra noted that the GDR had been a lifelong endeavor which is now *kaputt* (broken) for her parents' generation, which had also been betrayed under Nazism.

Petra received a termination notice from her teaching position because she had served as the SED secretary at her school. Following an appeal hearing, at which she pointed out that the pupils had chosen her the most trustworthy teacher in the school at the end of the 1990 academic year, she received permission to teach fifth and sixth grade pupils. Petra lamented, however, that she would not be able to teach older pupils as well since she very much enjoyed interacting with teenagers. While she felt relieved that she would have employment for the immediate future, she feared that eventually her position might be terminated for one of a variety of reasons, including her PDS membership. Petra claimed that many people left the PDS because they feared membership may have endangered their career opportunities in the new Germany. She even considered the possibility of teaching on a Native American reserve in Canada as a way of making a new life for herself and her son, who like many other East German children grew up with the adventure stories of Karl May and is very fond of Native Americans. Fortunately, she obtained a teaching position at a *Gymnasium* (a university preparatory high school) at the beginning of the 1994-95 academic year, prompting her to feel much more secure about her future. She has even made a couple of visits to the United States which provided her with opportunities to improve her English.

Although commentators such as Guenther Grass had characterized the GDR as a "niche society," Petra maintains that East Germans have retreated even more into their private worlds, in part because many of them cannot afford the higher price of eating out and entertainment. Whereas the GDR provided her with monthly child support payments of 95 Marks, the FRG in 1991 provided her only with 50 Marks. Because of the increase of criminality, including physical assaults, she purchased her father's Lada in order to avoid the danger of riding the subway. Later on she purchased a Western automobile.

Petra felt that the merger of the two Germanies was not an authentic unification but rather a colonization in which the stronger power imposes its will upon the weaker one. She lamented that the positive features of the GDR, such as its recycling system and its sick leave policy, had been dismantled along with its negative aspects.

For a while Petra was active in the Lichtenberg chapter of *Linke Frauen* (Leftist Women), a PDS affiliate, but ceased attending meetings in part due to increased work demands. She admires many of the ideals and objectives of the alternative political groups in East Germany, but laments their tendency to distance themselves from PDS, a posture which she finds understandable given that their members protested against the policies of the SED leadership whereas the vast majority of rank-and-file SED members did not. While Petra admires Gregor Gysi, the former chairperson of PDS, she fears that internal divisions and external factors may work against the success of the party. Despite the collapse of the GDR, she still believes that democratic socialism is needed to eradicate global patterns of economic exploitation, massive social inequality, and destruction of the environment.

The Lives of Other Former SED Members after the Wende

Michael's Life in the New Germany

Michael, whom we encountered in Chapter 3, maintained that in contrast to the hopefulness that East Germans felt when the Wall was opened in October 1989, most of them now feel frustrated. He noted that the degree of disillusionment with life in the new Germany varies from person to person, but is perhaps most severe for elderly people. Michael felt that most East Germans were materially better off in early 1991 than they were before the Wende, but noted that very few felt that their jobs were secure. He stated: "We still have our old rents and transportation fares and there have been some increases in salaries. I pay less for food than before the Wende." Michael said that many East Germans went into debt when they purchased Western automobiles (both new and old), often at inflated prices. He said many East Germans escape from the realities of the unification by watching television and videos.

Michael did not regard Helmut Koehl as his chancellor. He stated: "We do not visit the West often. We are used to the East sector." His wife, also a former SED member and a school teacher, added: "When we drive to West Berlin, we feel like we are in a different world and are glad when we return to East Berlin." Michael argued that many East Germans took the amenities of GDR society for granted. He felt that East Germans are developing a GDR identity for the first time. Michael maintained that although the Wessis would like to maintain the status quo, the Ossis will not accept unemployment. Whereas West Germans tend to regard unemployment as a personal problem, East Germans view it as a structural one. In early 1991 Michael expected that riots might occur in East Germany within the next six months to a year.

Michael stated: "We in the SED hoped that could reform the SED after Honecker stepped down. We hoped that young people or reformers like Modrow would move into positions of leadership." He added: "I had hoped that the unification would teach the world something. I had hoped that we [East Germans] could have served as a link between East and West. We received many impulses from the East but we had a Western identity. Now we have that video stuff from the West [and noted that Video Center bought up many former recycling centers]." He felt that most East Germans were either indifferent or opposed to the Gulf War and lamented that both the FRG and GDR had supported the development of Saddam Hussein's arsenal, noting that FRG firms had sold chemical weapons to Iraq and that Czechoslovakia had built a chemical warfare combat training camp there. Although Michael was a PDS member for a while, he resigned from the party as a result of a scandal involving the smuggling of funds to the Soviet Union. He felt that PDS lacks grass-roots support, but noted that many young people in East Berlin are attracted to the party.

Michael felt that the East German CDU merely changed one master for another. He said that it accepted socialist ideals and the SED as the leading party, despite its criticism of the SED. Michael maintained that some CDU members were more dogmatic leftists than many SED members. He said that people who belonged to the CDU and the other bloc parties in GDR society may sometimes have had an easier time establishing a career because the former had relatively few members whereas the SED had many. Michael characterized DeMaziere, the former leader of the East German CDU, and his government as a bunch of criminals and incompetents, many of whom had close connections with the Stasi.

Hannah's Life in the New Germany

During the Wende, Hannah, whom we also encountered in Chapter 3, came into contact with a group of social workers who worked for a women's shelter operated by the Catholic Church. Even though she belonged to the SED, the social workers accepted her. Hannah formed an English club with them in order to help them improve their English. For a while the club, which referred to itself as a human rights group, affiliated itself with New Forum. By early 1991 it had evolved into a support group. Hannah decided to leave SED because she felt that she had not joined it voluntarily. She sympathizes with the goals of Alliance 90 and the Greens. Hannah kept a small GDR flag in her study as a nostalgic memento of the positive features of the GDR. She expressed fear that Prenzlauer Berg may undergo gentrification, especially as West Germans reclaim former properties, and become a "chicy-mickey" area. Hannah added that many cafes have become prohibitively expensive for bohemians such as herself. Sometime during the first half of 1991, a review commission accused her of having been a Stasi collaborator. Instead of risking receiving a letter of dismissal, she resigned her teaching position at Humboldt University and accepted a job teaching English in West Berlin. Since 1991 Hannah has held a number of jobs doing translations and teaching English. In 1995 she split her time between two jobs, one in West Berlin and the other in the city of Brandenburg.

Thomas's Life in the New Germany

Thomas, whom we also encountered in Chapter 3, said that he left the SED because Modrow came out in favor of unification. He was not sure how his former SED membership would affect his job as the assistant director of his school, especially since he had attended a Parteischule (party school). Thomas referred to the Wende in its initial stages as a "happy, sometimes, comical revolution." He maintained that the GDR was sucked up by the FRG and that most East Germans were naive about how capitalism functions, pointing out that many of the people in Erfurt, where he had taught German to people from capitalist countries during the summers, believed that they would be rich one year after the currency exchange of July 1990. Prior to the Wende, he had managed to cut back to smoking only two cigarettes a day but started up again to cope with the stresses that the Wende and unification brought. He regarded West Germans as colonialists who are primarily interested in establishing new markets in East Germany. Conversely, he argued that West German companies intended to destroy the East German economy so that they can buy former GDR firms cheaply. Thomas personally did not know of anyone who was economically better off since the Wende, although he noted that some craftspeople were prospering due to the greater availability of supplies. He said that while many East Germans have taken trips to the West, most of them cannot afford to take such excursions any longer. The former West German owners of the Gartenhaus Thomas and his wife purchased for 56,000 Ostmarks have filed a claim to repossess it. In response he and his wife filed a complaint with the *Mieteschutz* (tenants' protection agency). He referred to the FRG social system as brutal and pointed out that life in East Berlin had become very dangerous at night, particularly in the vicinity of Bahnhof-Lichtenberg where neo-fascists had occupied several apartment buildings. Thomas stated that he had come to better appreciate the positive features of the GDR.

Thomas didn't feel that PDS had undergone a genuine reformation and that its policy of retaining its former holdings made it suspect in the eyes of many East Germans. He felt that PDS still had many hard-liners within its ranks and lacked the courage to be brutally honest about its past. While Gysi is a brilliant leader, he alone could not hold the party together. Michael referred to Egon Krenz, a former member of the Politburo who replaced Honecker briefly as General Secretary of the SED, as an "idiot" who unscrupulously sold his memoirs to the ultraconservative *Bild Zeitung*. He said whereas *Neues Deutschland* once was a propaganda sheet for the SED, it had become a good newspaper.

The Lives of East German Professionals Who Did Not Belong to the SED

Gertrude's Life in the New Germany

Gertrude, a woman in her sixties whom I interviewed in early 1991, was the head librarian in one of the units of the Humboldt University library system. Although she had never been married, she referred to the students who used her library as her "children." Over the years, Gertrude served as a surrogate-mother, counselor, academic advisor, and friend to scores of students. She once told me that the most important thing in life is to be a *Mensch* (decent person). Her West Berlin relatives repeatedly encouraged her to leave the GDR, both before and after the construction of the Wall, but Gertrude chose to remain. She said that she has always been an internationalist and anti-fascist. Despite her intense loyalty to the GDR, Gertrude never joined the SED and was a staunch critic of its leadership and the Stasi, which she referred to as a "state within a state." In commenting on one occasion upon the nature of the SED leadership, she satirically quoted George Orwell's passage in *Animal Farm*: "All pigs are equal, but some are more equal than others." Gertrude decided not to pursue graduate studies because she feared that she would have to censor herself. When students asked her what they could do about the decision of the SED in the fall of 1988 to ban *Sputnik*, Gertrude encouraged them to be patient because she believed that the GDR would eventually be transformed into a more humane society.

Gertrude did not expect that the unification would proceed as quickly as it did. She lamented that the GDR, despite all of its defects, had collapsed. Gertrude stated: "We achieved something in the GDR. We developed our agricultural system, fed ourselves (sometimes too well), and still exported food. How is that the Soviet Union with its land has been unable to develop a productive agricultural system? Russians thought that we in the GDR lived well." She felt that the GDR leadership elected in March 1990 sold the GDR out to the FRG and that it would have been better to have developed an authentically democratic socialist society in the GDR after the Wende. Gertrude noted that Russia and Eastern European countries cannot afford to purchase East German products any longer because they lack the necessary D-Marks. She complained that whereas the FRG experienced a boom due to new markets in East Germany, the latter had been forced to cut back on production. Conversely. Gertrude asserted that most West Germans didn't want to support or subsidize the development of East Germany. She feared that unemployment, demoralization, and health problems would plague East Germans, noting that Germans like to work and that the nerve clinics are already overflowing with patients.

Robert's Life in the New Germany

Robert is an instructor in his late fifties at Humboldt University who decided not to pursue a dissertation B (a second doctorate known as the *Habilitation*) because he did not want to play party games in the SED. He told me in November 1988 that he felt that he had been passed over for certain academic awards, including travel to the West, because he was not a SED member. Ironically, since he was not a member of the SED, he had become relatively secure in his position. Robert said that 70 to 75 percent of the university staff belonged to the SED and that close connections existed between the university administration and the Stasi. He added that "our system taught us to distrust people." After the unification, Robert joined the *Oeffentliche Transport und Verkehr Gewerkschaft* (Open Transport and Traffic Union), a FRG-based union that successfully negotiated to increase the salaries of East German teachers to 60 percent of their West German counterparts after June 1991. Some university employees joined the more leftist *Gewerkschaft fuer Erziehung und Wissenschaft* (Union for Socialization and Science).

Robert took part in the euphoric events of the Wende. When Gorbachev's motorcade drove down Schoenhauser Alle near his apartment in October 1989, he held up a placard that read in English. "Mr. Gorbachev, your philosophy of socialism is our great power." His colleague held up a placard that read, "Wo ist unser Gorby?" (Where is our Gorby?). Because placards had been forbidden when Soviet dignitaries visited the GDR in the past, people in the area where Robert and his colleague stood applauded when they held up their placards. Whereas some Soviet officials smiled when they saw the placards, Robert said that the GDR policeman in the last car in the motorcade looked at them disapprovingly. Although he feared that he and his colleague might be arrested for their actions, they were not.

Robert felt in early 1991 that if the socioeconomic situation in East Germany worsened, more East Germans would protest but over the long run most would seek individualistic solutions to their problems, particularly since socialism as an alternative to capitalism had been discredited both philosophically and existentially. He estimated that only 5 to 10 percent of East Germans actually believed in the ideals of socialism.

He maintained that the protests thus far have lacked theoretical consistency and clear-cut objectives. Conversely, Robert observed that East Germans don't want to be second-class citizens and probably will protest for strictly economistic goals as workers generally have in other developed capitalist countries. He himself supports the SPD since it promotes social benefits for workers within the context of a welfare capitalist system.

Sylvia's Life in the New Germany

Sylvia is a language teacher at a Volkshochschule in East Berlin. She never belonged to the SED but voted for Alliance 90 candidates in the elections of March and December 1990. She lives in a house with her partner and son who is a university student. During the Wende, her colleagues voted out the former head, who had been a SED member, of the language department and elected her to this position. Sylvia also serves as the assistant director of the school which concentrates largely on the teaching of language courses.

Like other educational institutions in East Germany, unification translated into immense adjustments for her school. While she found it gratifying to work with her counterparts in West Berlin, Sylvia also has found the process frustrating and stressful in that "We [East Germans] have to adapt to their profile." Indeed, many West German policies, not only in the area of education, reminded her of colonialism. She felt that the former GDR was being absorbed rather than integrated into the FRG. Whereas West Berlin Volkshochschulen offered classes 30 weeks a year and functioned almost exclusively with part-time instructors or "freelancers," those in the GDR offered courses 38 weeks a year and functioned primarily with both full-time instructors and part-time instructors (about 20 of the former and about 50 of the latter at Sylvia's Hochschule). Sylvia said that West Berlin Volkshochschulen tend to concentrate on hobby or "tra-a-la-la" courses while GDR ones provided their graduates with language certification for employment. [Other types of West German schools provide language certification.] In contrast to the hierarchical structure of West Berlin Volkshochschulen and despite the authoritarian structure of the GDR state, she felt that GDR Volkshochschulen allowed for more input from faculty. She felt that FRG office settings require more formal dress standards of their employees than did those in the GDR. Sylvia maintained that the FRG bureaucracy is more unwieldy than the GDR bureaucracy was. At the end of the 1990-91 academic year, all of the full-time teaching positions at Sylvia's Volkshochschule were terminated.

During the first half of 1991, Sylvia earned around 1,800 Marks per month. Although her monthly salary was about 400 Marks higher than during the Wende, her taxes had increased significantly under the FRG system. She said that assistant directors of the Hochschulen in West Berlin earned around 5,000 Marks per month. Sylvia said that postal rates for regular letters had increased from 20 Pfenning to 50 Pfenning. In early 1991, it cost her two Marks instead of one Mark to go swimming at the local *Schimmhalle* (indoor swimming pool).

Sylvia said that serious tensions had developed between Wessis and Ossis. She said that some West Berliners said that an Ossi may be identified by cheap jeans, bad smell, and patterned tights in the case of women. East Germans refer to East Germany as "Koehl's Plantation" and many West Germans said, "The Ossis should first roll up their arm sleeves and work properly rather than always complain."

Her son, Peter, who studied sociology for a while at the Free University in West Berlin, asserted that he found it easier to become acquainted with Ossi than Wessi students. He noted that many of his former East German colleagues were studying sociology in order to better understand the process of social change in East Germany. Peter maintained that most Ossi university students did not favor unification but rather supported Alliance 90 and even PDS during the Wende. He observed that many students had shifted from using phrases such as *Scheiss Osten* ("shitty East") and *Scheiss Sozialismus* ("shitty socialism") to express their alienation from GDR society to a serious analysis of socialist and anarchist concepts. Peter eventually decided to drop his studies in sociology because he felt that he would not be employable after obtaining a degree in it.

Veronica's Life in the New Germany

In early 1991 Veronica taught German and English in an Oberschule in Pankow. She and her husband, Manfred (a brewery worker whom we will meet in the next section), live in a relatively spacious apartment in Pankow within easy access of the U-Bahn (subway) station. Although many East Berliners regard Pankow as the most pleasant Stadtbezirk of East Berlin, many young couples chose to leave the generally small Altbau apartments there for the larger apartments with central heating in the Neubau areas of the city. Despite the fact that Veronica never belonged to the SED, she admitted that she identified with the GDR system and had been naive about many of its shortcomings. Unlike many East Germans, she wasn't particularly dissatisfied with her material standard of living in the GDR, in part because she valued social relations more than material things. Veronica still believed that in theory socialism is a more equitable system than capitalism, but came to believe that the former isn't achievable because humans are not sufficiently committed to make it work. She experienced an existential crisis in that she did not feel that she had subscribed to any concrete philosophy.

Although Veronica did not have any immediate fear of losing her teaching position, she feared that her husband might lose his job at the brewery, noting that East Germans of their generation had never experienced unemployment. In order to secure her teaching position, she had begun to study French. Veronica felt depressed about the socioeconomic situation in East Germany and did not feel that demonstrations against the new system were being effective. Unfortunately, her mother, a movie theater employee, was in danger of losing her job because so few East Germans were now attending movie theaters. In contrast to the GDR system, workers in the new system were not asked whether they want to perform a particular task at their place of employment. Due to the wide variety of brand names available and the "specials" in the new Germany, Veronica felt that one had to spend more time shopping in order to find a bargain. Nevertheless, she observed that the price of bread had gone up from 90 Pfenning to 1.90 Marks. Her family had paid 36 Marks for a meal out, whereas the same meal would have previously cost them half as much in the GDR. Despite the greater availability of consumer goods, Veronica commented, "I don't see happiness in the population." She noted that beginning in the fall of 1991, parents would have to pay fees for children attending Kindergarten. Veronica lamented that some hospitals and polyclinics in East Germany had been closed and stated that the good parts of the GDR system, such as the polyclinics, were being destroyed in the unification process.

In October 1990 she had visited the United States on a trip for school teachers arranged by the German-North American Friendship Society (a private company started by the former secretary of the former state-sponsored GDR-USA Friendship Society). She confessed to having believed that America is an evil place prior to her visit. Even though this notion was dispelled, Veronica obtained the impression during her week-long visit that most Americans have little time for each other. She stayed in the Milwaukee home of an African-American teacher with a thirteen-year-old daughter. Veronica felt that this woman and her daughter did not even eat a "real breakfast" before they left home for the day. Although she found Americans friendly, at least in a superficial manner, the ones she met in Milwaukee did not evince any interest in East Germany.

Frau Huber's Life in the New Germany

In 1991 Inga Huber was the sole representative of the *Deutsche Soziale Union* (DSU or German Social Union) in *Stadtbezirk Mitte* (Central City District) of East Berlin, which she described as a former SED-stronghold because of its concentration of middle-level state functionaries. According to Hamilton,

> The Christian Social Union was forged in late January 1990 out of twelve existing political parties and opposition groupings with the direct assistance and support of the conservative West German Christian Social Union (CSU). The CSU immediately proclaimed the DSU its East German partner and offered electoral assistance. The DSU in turn called for immediate unification. The DSU was the product of fears by West German conservatives that the tacit truce that had been established between conservative and social democratic opposition groups would result in defeat of conservative forces in the GDR election (Hamilton 1990:20).

Frau Huber said that prior to the Wende she eschewed political involvement. For the most part, she had been a traditional Hausfrau (housewife) and wife of a physician employed at the Charity, the university hospital in East Berlin. Frau Huber maintained that her husband had been denied professorial status because he did not belong to the SED. During the Wende, however, she concluded that it was not enough to complain and began to study the programs of the various political parties. Frau Huber decided that the DSU had the most attractive program and was also attracted to it because it did not have any members who had been East German CDU collaborators with the GDR state. She comes from a Social Democratic family and her grandfather was a KPD member. Frau Huber stated that Marxist theory is good but that its application had been repressive. She was committed to socialist ideals until the GDR state's suppression of the workers' rebellion in 1953. As a consequence, she decided not to join the SED.

Although she retains social democratic tendencies due to her socialization, Frau Huber joined the conservative DSU because she wanted to be part of the effort to depose the SED regime. Although she intended to leave politics upon expiration of her term in 1992, she felt that holding political office has greatly enhanced her political consciousness. Frau Huber stated that although the DSU is in coalition with the CDU and more or less subscribed to its political agenda, the former didn't want any East German CDU members within its ranks. Conversely, she argued that although the mainstream of the DSU wanted to distance itself from the Republican Party, some DSU members exhibited neo-fascist tendencies as well.

As opposed to its strength in the South of East Germany, the DSU is in a distinct minority in the Bezirk Stadtmitte (center city)-a district dominated by the PDS and Alliance 90. Of the 85 representatives in 1991, about 37 belonged to PDS, 20 to SPD, 14 to CDU, 11 to Alliance 90, two to a small party called *Wir Frauen* (We Women), and one to the *Nelken* (Carnations)-a group that was "formed by members of the SED in mid-January [1990] as a socialist party whose platform would integrate the writings of German revolutionaries Karl Liebknecht and Rosa Luxemburg, with those of Marx, Engels, and Lenin" (Hamilton 1990:40). Frau Huber maintained that an informal alliance of PDS and Alliance 90 dominated the Rathaus and added that in order to avoid being labeled a power grabbing party, PDS had allowed Alliance 90 to exert more influence than it actually had. For example, although PDS could have occupied the mayoral office, the mayor of the Stadtmitte was a former member of New Forum. Frau Huber maintained that Alliance 90 came to distrust the mayor because he came to view himself as a king.

Although Frau Huber belonged to a conservative party which is in coalition with the CDU and CSU, her visit to the ministries of economics and social affairs in Bonn convinced her that government bureaucrats lack an understanding for the social problems in East Germany. She also complained that some 80 percent of the Treuhand employees were former SED members and that members of Modrow's government gave themselves raises in the last days of the GDR because they expected that they would be laid off.

Georg and Ruth's Lives in the New Germany

From 5 April to 7 April 1991, I revisited my cousin, Georg Nachtwei, and his wife, Ruth, in Magdeburg. Whereas Georg's firm was formerly a division of a Leipzig-based state combine, it had become an independent heating equipment firm with some 1,500 employees in Magdeburg. Georg had become the head of the firm's planning office with thirty employees. Whereas he had earned 1,500 Marks a month before the Wende, his salary had risen to 4,000 a month.

Ruth had become an employee of Karstadt, an Essen-based department store chain that took over the *Centrum*-the former state department store in Magdeburg. In March 1991 she attended a four-week training workshop in Hannover in which she learned Karstadt's bookkeeping system. Whereas her place of employment had some 1,200 employees prior to the Wende, its work force under Karstadt's management had been downsized to 700 - 800.

Unlike many East Germans, Georg and Ruth felt relatively financially secure. Georg noted that his company, which continued to sell heating equipment to the Soviet Union, might go broke, particularly if the Soviet Union (now the Commonwealth of Independent States) could not continue to pay for products in hard currency. If he would be laid off, he would receive 63 percent of his salary. Georg said that he and Ruth couldn't complain about their financial situation, but noted that they may face difficulties if prices would increase more rapidly than their salaries.

Overall, Georg and Ruth were satisfied with the unification process and voted for the CDU in the 1990 elections. While he felt that the SPD has a better social policies than the CDU, he maintained that the latter had better economic policies. Georg stated: "Koehl has made some mistakes but Honecker made only mistakes. Honecker is responsible for the problems in East Germany, not Koehl." He felt that Honecker and Mielke, the former Stasi head, were criminals and that it was prudent for East Germany to separate itself from the Soviet Union quickly. He maintained that many former SED leaders holding positions in firms, police departments, and even the Treuhand were attempting to sabotage the new system.

Georg, however, maintained that if West German politicians failed to support the development of the East Germany economy, East Germany would evolve into a *Kolonie* (colony), thus forcing East Germans to resist their enslavement. He said that when he told a West German producer that his company should help renovate the East German economy, the producer replied that he could earn more profits by producing in the West and selling his products in the East. Georg feels that the FRG must adopt some of the positive features of the GDR social system, such as more liberal laws on abortion. Georg asserted that a significant increase in crime has occurred since the Wende in East Germany. He complained that the police didn't stop speeders and looked the other way when neo-Nazis attacked an apartment squatted by "leftists" in Magdeburg. A by-standing police officer reportedly stated that he could not enforce order for a meager wage of 750 Marks a month.

Georg said that whereas the "end of the world" once was 40 kilometers west of Magdeburg (the former GDR-FRG border crossing near Helmstadt), the Wende brought him and his wife access to a whole new world. In addition to having made numerous trips to West Germany, by 1991 he and Ruth had vacationed in France and Austria. Nevertheless, they felt uncomfortable upon visiting the Ku'damm area of West Berlin. After two hours of seeing poor people, beggars, and AIDS victims, they went to Alexanderplatz in East Berlin where they felt more comfortable.

The Lives of East German Workers after the Wende

The Lives of East German Brewers in the New Germany

I first became acquainted with three brewery workers - David, Manfred, and Wolfgang - at a Country Western dance in January 1989. They all worked in the cleaning and disinfection department of an East Berlin brewery that prior to the Wende exported its best beer to the West. I visited Manfred and Wolfgang and their families in their apartments both before and after the Wende. In March 1991 I spent several hours visiting them and several of their fellow workers at the brewery.

Prior to the Wende Manfred told me that there was not enough democracy in the GDR. He had served as a border guard for a year, but hated the Wall. Manfred and his wife had never belonged to the SED. He stated that the SED leadership was hypocritical in that it preached that it drank water but actually drank wine. Manfred noted that the GDR state's slogan, *"Alles fuer das Volk"* ("Everything for the people"), was contradicted by the reality that "one had to run around for every piece of dirt." He maintained that the GDR economy was inefficient, noting that "We had to invent substitutes for parts that should have been purchased."

When I visited Manfred again in mid-February 1991, he told me that he welcomed the Wende and thought that the socioeconomic situation in East Germany would improve eventually, although he was not sure exactly how soon this would occur. He also admitted that East Germany would remain a poor region of Germany for a long time. He stated that socialism was an impossible dream and that capitalism is the only economic system that functions effectively, even though it is not a particularly "nice" system. After the unification, the brewery had been taken over by a West German company and was producing at 40 to 50 percent of its former output. Manfred was not sure if he would remain employed and observed that "I don't know what it is like to be unemployed." He added that he was willing to work for low wages for five years or so with the hope that his wages would increase after the East German economy underwent renovation. He admitted that he had less work to do at his job than before the Wende. Manfred said that although he sometimes found his work boring, his job generally had been a source of satisfaction for him.

Although about ten years younger than Manfred, Wolfgang had been even more dissatisfied with the GDR state. He noted, however, that he liked his job at the brewery. He felt optimistic about the future of East Germany and complained that many East Germans focused excessively on the negative aspects of the unification. Wolfgang noted that although East Germans had been dissatisfied with the two-to-one currency exchange (after the first 4,000 Marks for adults and 2,000 Marks for children) in July 1990, they would have been happy to have exchanged at this rate prior to the Wende. He contended that if the GDR had continued to have existed, it would have ended up in an economic situation similar to that of Poland. While Wolfgang did not feel that unemployment was a pleasant status, he argued that East German workers should restrain their animosity toward the new system and should not expect wages on par with their West German counterparts immediately. Nevertheless, he admitted that Western corporations tend to treat their workers as instruments in their drive to earn profits. Michael admitted that one negative consequence of the unification has been an increase of traffic in East Berlin. He and his wife did not feel that they could allow their daughter and son to play outside for this reason.

When I visited the brewery, the Chef of the cleaning and disinfection department noted his pessimism about the future of East Germany and his disappointment with the unwillingness of West German labor unions to provide more support to East German workers. A 55-year-old worker stated that he did not feel that he would have any job prospects if he were laid off from his present position. A younger worker said that while his family's material standard of living had improved since the Wende, this would only be the case so long as he and his wife remained employed. A fourth worker observed, "We are brewers and can only work as brewers" and a fifth worker referred to brewers as *Fachidioten* (trade idiots). A young female worker, who was slated to work as a trainee for another year, confessed uncertainty about the future of her position but felt that she must try to be optimistic about the future.

At lunch I spoke at length with David, who had been placed in charge of the production control department. He argued that East Germans were generally better off after than before the Wende. David lamented that East Germans complained because they were economically worse off than West Germans, but argued that they had forgotten the negative aspects of the GDR state and remember only its positive aspects. He said that East Germans obtained spiritual freedom after the unification whereas the GDR state suppressed their individuality and made them schizophrenic. David maintained that the Marxian notion of socialism is an utopian ideal which runs counter to human nature. He argued that only a benevolent dictatorship could ensure the development of an ideal society. Whereas most of the workers in his department voted for the SPD, he voted for the CDU in the elections of 1990.

Helmut's Life in the New Germany

Helmut is a *Schlosser* (locksmith) in his late twenties who began to work in late 1990 for a small firm that installs windows in buildings. In early 1991 he lived with his wife, a school teacher, in a Pankow apartment. Helmut learned his trade in a state firm and worked with a group of "antisocial" people who often chose not to report for work. He felt that he had to work harder at this new place of employment than at the state firm, but had run into difficulties with his immediate Chef, a friend whose father owned the firm.

Helmut was uncertain as to how much longer he and his wife would be employed. In anticipation of possible unemployment, they were trying to pull together their resources. Although he felt that he and his wife would manage to survive, he worried about the future of his parents' generation. Helmut said that one often sees want ads asking that only individuals under 35 years of age apply for positions. While he felt that the socioeconomic situation in East Germany would improve in the next five years, he argued that the FRG government should take care of the older workers who were losing their positions. Helmut stated that West Germany underwent a second economic miracle as result of the unification and is profiting from East Germany. He felt that the FRG was destroying the East German economy and resented the West German expression that "everything from the East is dung."

While Helmut felt in early 1991 that he could possibly find employment in West Berlin, he continued to work in the East out of a sense of loyalty to it. He stated, "I am an East Berliner and am proud of it. I was born in Pankow and am proud of Pankow." Helmut resented the

West German stereotype of East Germans that asserted: "*Man ist nichts: man kann nichts. man weisst nichts*" ("They are nothing; they can't do anything; they don't know anything"). He added. "We can learn skills. If something is broken, we fix it ourselves whereas they can't repair it." Helmut maintained that GDR schools were better at teaching writing skills than were the West Berlin schools. He argued: "What the West Germans learn in the sixth grade, the East Germans learned in the fourth grade."

According to Helmut, East Germans lived quietly and had jobs prior to the Wende, but afterwards their lives became hectic and uncertain, even if they could much more easily buy bananas. He said that after the unification East Germans had to spend a lot of their time seeking bargains in order to make their low incomes stretch. He and his wife shopped in West Berlin every Friday just so that they could live within their means since prices had become higher in East Berlin. Helmut also felt that East Germans had far less time for socializing than they did before the Wende. He said that his friendship circle had contracted to a third of what it had been before the Wende. Helmut feared that East Germans had adopted the West German pattern of "*jeder fuer sich*" ("everyone for himself or herself"). He felt that conversations came to focus on questions such as "How will I make it?" and "How can I make the most money?" Helmut and his wife felt exhausted upon coming home in the evening and generally unwound by talking and drinking tea. He had been so preoccupied with the changes in East Germany that he did not have time to think about freedom and added that he lacked the money and time to feel freer.

Helmut disliked the CDU and preferred the SPD which he regarded to be an *Arbeiterpartei* (workers' party). He maintained that a sound social policy for East Germany would include portions from each of the various party's programs. While Helmut supported *Umweltpolitik* (environmental politics), he accused the Greens of wanting a high standard of living while opposing nuclear power. He agreed with many of their ideas, but felt that the Greens presented themselves poorly by wearing dirty clothes in the Bundestag. Helmut had mixed feelings about the potential of socialism. He argued that the GDR had only a rudimentary form of socialism and believes that in theory socialism is a better system than capitalism. Helmut felt that the development of socialism would be impossible in the short run, but believed that it could occur within the next 500 years. Conversely, he believed that communism is an impossible utopian ideal that cannot be realized because some people will always want more than others.

Roland's Life in the New Germany

Roland is a young single worker who in 1991 lived in Bernau, a small city north of East Berlin. Even though he was on Kurzarbeit (short-work) at the time, he felt that social conditions had improved in East Germany since the Wende. Roland said that he was in favor of German unification and anticipated some of the present problems in East Germany. Although he felt that he had lived comfortably prior to the Wende, Roland stated that his life had improved since the Wende due to the greater availability of consumer products and freedom to travel in the West as well as to express his opinions openly. Prior to the Wende, Roland earned about 900 to 1,100 Marks *netto* (wages after deductions), but his wages rose to 1,250 to 1,400 Marks netto after the Wende until he became a Kurzarbeiter, for which he received 63 percent of his regular wages. He occasionally worked part-time for a West Berlin company.

In addition to his job for a GDR state firm that installed heating systems in factories, schools and dwelling units, Roland worked privately prior to the Wende. Although he and his fellow workers often had to wait long periods of time for materials, this situation posed an intellectual challenge for them in that they had to make or find substitute parts. In contrast, he felt that his work since the Wende had become been more mundane and strenuous at times. Roland described himself as a flexible person who would like to eventually leave the East Berlin area, especially if Berlin would be chosen as the site of Olympics in the year 2000 because it would become an even more hectic place. He said that he would like to earn a little more money, but wasn't going to worry about it. Roland readily admitted that he has youth on his side since he could easily look for work elsewhere.

Prior to the Wende, Roland belonged to both the Young Pioneers and FDJ for what he termed opportunistic reasons. He left FDJ in 1986 because its leaders criticized an essay in which he remarked that whereas the German youth wore brown shirts during the Nazi period, the GDR youth wore blue shirts. He refused to study Russian in school as a protest against the GDR state. Roland argued that there was a difference between socialism in theory and in reality in the GDR and cited a DDR Witz (GDR joke) that stated: "*Dass ist nicht Sozialismus. Dass ist Delikatismus*" ("This is not socialism. This is Delikatism"). He referred to the shops, which had sold higher quality goods at considerably higher prices with Ostmarks, on *Leipziger Strasse* in the center of East Berlin as the best example of Delikatismus. Roland contended that Marxism-Leninism is a utopian ideology because it overlooks human nature. He voted for the

SPD in the March 1990 election because it had better social policies than the CDU, but crossed out all of the candidates in the December 1990 election as a form of protest. Although he felt that Alliance 90 had some good ideas, Roland maintained that overall it was too utopian, such as, for example, in its initial desire to maintain the GDR and its proposal to dismantle the German army.

The Response of East Berlin Pupils and Teachers to the Unification

In early 1991, I was invited to speak in several English classes in two Oberschulen in East Berlin. On 26 February I visited "Vincent Poroinbha" Oberschule in Lichtenberg, the school at which Petra Preussler taught. She told me that the GDR had an approved list from which schools could draw their namesake. When I told her that I had seen an "Angela Davis" Oberschule in the small city of Wittenberg in Sachsen-Anhalt, she noted that Angela Davis was an important cultural figure in the GDR. Petra added that the famous Cuban revolutionary, Che Guevara, was not on the approved list. Under the GDR educational system, the lower level of an Oberschule consisted of grades one through four whereas the upper level consisted of grades five through ten or five through twelve, depending on the school. Vincent Porointha Oberschule or School 445 was slated to become a *Grundschule* (elementary school) in September 1991 in accordance with the FRG educational system.

The first class that I visited consisted of eighth graders who had been studying English for one-and-one-half years. Although I started out by speaking in English, I switched to German because the pupils were self-conscious about speaking in English. The pupils in this class asked me about my hobbies, my children, and my favorite sports. The second class that I met was the fifth grade group which proved to be the most excited about my visit. Many of the pupils in this group greeted me personally before class and were the most uninhibited of the three classes in attempting to speak English, even though it was only in its first year of English language training. At the beginning of class, they sang a song titled "My Friend Superman." The third class was an eighth grade group which initially was the shyest of the three groups, but they gradually opened up. Pupils in all of the classes mentioned the wider selection of consumer products as a positive feature of the unification and unemployment and higher prices as negative features of the unification. Many pupils in the eighth grade group felt that life was better in East Germany prior to the unification. When I asked which of the political parties offered the best program for East Germany, one student said that the FDP did, but could not give a reason for his response. While only one pupil expressed support for the PDS, none of them exhibited overt support for the CDU. When I asked if there is a need for a new party, one pupil suggested a *Kindernpartei* (children's party).

During the breaks, I briefly spoke with two female teachers in their thirties. One of them expressed annoyance with West German women who believe that East Germans are lazy. She said that West Germans are more pretentious than East Germans and maintained East Germans are warmer and more willing to admit their shortcomings than West Germans are. While she felt that the unification was necessary, she did not want it to be a unilateral process. The other teacher complained about the lack of recycling containers in East Berlin after the unification. She also argued that while teachers were not free to express their opinions prior to the Wende, they also were not free to do so under the FRG.

On 13 March I visited a ninth grade English class at an Oberschule in Pankow. Most of the nine pupils present did not seem impressed with the quality of life in East Germany since the Wende. A boy wearing long hair and a T-shirt with the letters CCCP (the Russian abbreviation for the USSR) and a hammer-and-sickle said that he wanted to move to Sweden. He asked me if American pupils and students are divided into leftists and rightists. A clean-cut looking blonde headed boy stated that he favors the Republican Party, apparently because he felt that foreigners were depriving Germans, including ones in the East, of jobs. A girl described life in East Germany after the Wende as *beschissen* (shitty).

Frau Schmidt (pseudonym) said that she had been teaching at the Oberschule since 1964, but she began her teaching career in 1949 at age 16. She felt that if the "old men" in the SED leadership had stepped down, the GDR may have succeeded. Frau Schmidt complained that the non-SED teachers, such as herself, were expected to follow the directions of the SED teachers. She complained that some of the same teachers who formerly taught *Staattbuergerkunde* (civics) under the GDR system are now teaching *Gesellschaftkunde* (social studies) under the new system. Despite her harsh criticisms of the GDR state, which she described as a dictatorship rather than authentic socialism, Frau Schmidt asserted that capitalism exploits people, the FRG system is designed to benefit rich people, and that the CDU is indifferent to the plight of the poor. She regretted that many of the pupils completing Oberschule had been unable to find an apprenticeship.

Assessments of East Germans on Their Current Situation and Their Future Prospects

This chapter has examined the views of various East Germans, some of whom belonged to the SED and others who did not, on life in East Germany after the Wende and during the first year following the German unification. It is difficult to say how representative the subjects I have included in this chapter were of the mood of East Germans throughout the new German states, particularly since most of my subjects were East Berliners where social amenities had been and continue to be better than in other regions of East Germany. Undoubtedly, this will continue to be the case because the Bundestag selected Berlin was as the new capital of united Germany in June 1991. Whereas East Berlin served as the showcase of the former German Democratic Republic, united Berlin will once again become the showcase of united Germany.

At any rate, most of the East Germans I interviewed spoke of massive dislocation in their lives and those of their relatives, friends, and acquaintances. Middle-aged and elderly subjects tended to express the greatest fear for the future whereas some of my younger subjects cautiously expressed hope that their lives would slowly, but steadily, improve. Other sources strongly suggest that their assessments of life in the new Germany are by no means atypical. Rosenberg assessed the mood of Germans in general during the months following the unification as follows:

With political unification achieved and joint elections held, life in Germany has not settled back into comfortably familiar patterns. In fact, reporting on the German unification process has shifted from reiterations of matter-of-factness of the whole thing to a growing consciousness of a barely concealed crisis. A recent survey by the Institute of Applied Social Research (INFAS) found that 83 percent of the former GDR citizens and 7 percent of the former West German (FRG) citizens felt that the situation in the five new states was "dramatic." In addition, 62 percent of eastern Germans and 59 percent of western Germans were "mostly" or "very" dissatisfied with developments since unification (Rosenberg 1991:141).

Many of my subjects stated that their socioeconomic situation in early 1991 had improved in the sense that they now had access to a variety of consumer goods and opportunities that they had not had in the GDR. Indeed, when questioned in a poll conducted by the *Berliner Zeitung* about the status of their personal situation one year after the 18 March 1990 election, 22.4 percent of the respondents answered that it was worse, 38.7 percent that it was better, 35.9 percent that it had not changed appreciably (or that it was better in some ways and worse in other ways), and 3.0 percent that they could not determine whether they were better or worse off (*Berliner Zeitung,* March 15, 1991). These statistics, however, did not reveal the pervasive uncertainty that most of my subjects expressed about their futures, particularly in terms of whether or not they would be able to retain their jobs. Indeed, *Newsweek* better captured the mood of East Germans by reporting:

> People in the east have ridden an 18-month roller coaster from the depths of Stalinism to the peak of liberation and down again to economic depression. They are now experiencing a collective case of what the Germans rather vaguely call Existenzangst-existential anxiety. Strikes, crime and suicides are spreading, and some of the tensio has spilled over into violence: in Dresden last week, right-wing soccer fans attacked players and fans from a visiting Yugoslav team (*Newsweek,* 1 April 1991, p. 28).

By early April 1991, conditions in East Germany and tensions between Ossis and Wessis had deteriorated sufficiently to prompt FRG Chancellor Helmut Koehl to make an unannounced trip to Erfurt in Thuringia to reassure East Germans that their socioeconomic situation would dramatically improve over the next several years.

Chapter 7

The Opposition in the New German States: Alliance 90, United Left, and the Party of Democratic Socialism

Over the course of the 1980s, various grass roots opposition groups, many of which found a sanctuary within the East German Evangelical church, emerged in the GDR. These included the New Konkret Committee for Peace (est. 1984), Initiative for Peace and Human Rights (est. 1985), the Working Group for a Church of Solidarity (est. 1986), the Environmental Library (est. 1986), the Church from Below (est. 1988), and the Ark-Green-ecological network (est. 1988). By the spring of 1989, numerous opposition groups existed in the GDR. Other groups were striving to unify and coordinate the various opposition groups on a nationwide basis. Most members were between 25 and 40 years of age and tended to be highly educated. Although nearly 100,000 people participated in some capacity in the opposition movement, the Stasi reported the presence of some 2,500 permanent activists and a 60-strong "hard core". At any rate, the opposition movement that played an instrumental role during the Wende had a different conception of what the future of the GDR should be than that of the East German masses. Many of its members favored, at least initially, the continuation of the GDR as a separate German state - one which would be sensitive to social needs and democratic and ecological ideals.

This chapter discusses the role of several successor organizations of the grass-roots movement, particularly Alliance 90 and the United Left, in the new German states. My observations are based heavily upon interviews and conversations that I had with various representatives of the grass-roots movement as well as several of their meetings that I attended in 1991. This chapter also examines the efforts of the Party of Democratic Socialism (PDS) to come to grips with its SED past and to function as a partner in the political opposition, one that remains in large measure distrusted by the grass-roots groups by relying largely upon the observations of two scholars who once belonged to the SED.

The Grass-Roots Movement in the New German States

Many grass-roots groups obtained housing in a building which came to be called the House of Democracy (Haus der Demokratie) during the Wende. The House of Democracy, which is situated at 165 Friedrichstrasse (one block south of Unter den Linden and across the street from the Grand Hotel) and belongs to the PDS, serves as the headquarters for many grass-roots organizations, including New Forum, Democracy Now, Initiative for Peace and Human Rights, United Left, Independent Women's Association, Committee for Free Baltic States (Kommittee Freies Baltikum), and the West German-based German Communist Party (DKP or Deutsche Kommunistische Partei).

Torpey (1995) maintains that the activists who formed opposition groups during the GDR period were marginal and continue to be marginal in the new Germany. Nevertheless,

> the civil-rights campaigners have been largely undeterred by their inability to stir wide popular backing. They have carried forward into united Germany some, though by no means all, of the objectives they pursued before and during Communism's collapse. Chastened and stripped of many illusions by their contact with the West, they have sought to continue their "abortive revolution" under the conditions of an imported but serviceable parliamentary republic (Torpey 1995:105-106).

Alliance 90

In early February 1990 a coalition of three leading grass-roots organizations, namely New Forum, Democracy Now, and Initiative for Peace and Human Rights formed Alliance (*Buendnis*) 90. The Independent Women's Association and the United Left participated in the discussions, but decided not to join the new coalition (Hamilton 1990:30).

The alliance tends to eschew labels that pigeonhole it into one political category or another, as is manifested by the slogan on of its posters which reads "*Nicht Rechts! Nicht Links!*" (Not right! Not left!). Members of Alliance 90 cannot belong to other parties. In the March 1990 election, Alliance 90 received only 2.9 percent of the vote. The Alliance formed a party group (*Fraktion*) with the East German Greens initially in the GDR Volkskammer and later in the FRG Bundestag with the West German Greens.

In 1991 the eight representatives of the Fraktion consisted of Ingrid Koeppe (NF), Werner Schulz (NF), Konrad Weiss (DJ), Wolfgang Ullmann (DJ), Gerd Poppe (IFM), Klaus-Dieter Feige, Christina Schenk, and Vera Wollenberger.

New Forum

New Forum (*Neues Forum* or NF) was founded by a group of largely middle-aged, leftist intellectuals and defectors from the SED. According to Hamilton,

> The grass-roots movement was founded by 30 representatives from 11 of the 15 GDR districts on September 9, 1989, in Gruenheidee, the home of the late Robert Havemann, the prominent critic of East German Stalinism. In their manifesto of September 12, the founders declared that they did not want to go West, did not want Germany reunification, and did not want capitalism. Instead, they sought the "restructuring of the German Democratic Republic" toward a humane, democratic socialism (Hamilton 1990:32-33).

NF quickly obtained over 200,000 signatures for its founding manifesto (Joppke 1995:141). Baerbel Bohley, an East Berlin artist of some renown, served as a pivotal figure in the establishment of New Forum. She had earlier been a founding member of IFM. Bohley first challenged the GDR state when she opposed the induction of women in the military in the early 1980s (Fisher 1995:150). Along with a couple dozen or so other people, she participated in 1988 at the state rally commemorating the assassination of Rosa Luxemburg and Karl Libeknecht in 1919 in the unfurling of a banner which quoted the former's famous line stating: "Freedom is always the freedom of those who think differently." For her involvement, Bohley was exiled to the FRG. After a stay in Britain, state authorities permitted her to return to the GDR in 1989. NF opened its first office on 18 October 1989 in Leipzig. By November 1989 it had evolved into a mass-member organization with several hundred branches. NF initially opposed the unification of the two Germanies. It opened its ranks to SED members during the Wende and wanted to reform the GDR economy in cooperation with the state, workers, and citizens. Efforts by the GDR state to suppress NF did much to boost its popularity and prompted weekly demonstrations in Leipzig and other GDR cities. NF called for the well-known demonstration at the Stasi headquarters on Normanstrasse on 15 January 1990. Despite NF's popularity during the fall of 1989, it failed to fill the political vacuum left by the collapse of the SED. According to Rossman (1990:69), NF "consistently refused to make the transition to a membership party, remaining instead an amorphous organization led by an increasingly fractious cluster of intellectual personalities responsible to no one."

In late January 1990 at its founding congress, internal divisions within NF became apparent, with the centrist forces prevailing when "the congress officially endorse[d] the idea of German unity, which, they argue, should be decided in a popular referendum in both German states, and then take place gradually, with the East maintaining some form of sovereignty for several years" (Hamilton 1990:34). Jens Reich, a physician who became the most prominent figure within NF, describes its decline as follows:

> In the months after the fall of the Wall and during its first free elections, New Forum was swept aside in the stampede towards unification. Other political parties were formed, each with its counterpart in West Germany, and they ran a merciless electoral campaign. In December 1989, they assured us that we would be allowed to develop our own East German form of democracy. It became rapidly clear that we would not. But you cannot stand against a dam breaking. And the political dam broke on the 9th of November with the Wall. The West German Chancellor Helmut Koehl was not unhappy at the breakneck pace of developments. His interest was quite obvious. He forged ahead by all means, seeing that if he lost momentum, everyone in Europe would begin to discuss the German question, to enter reservations, demand conditions and slow things down. He therefore tried to exploit the momentum

of the moment. Hence his public espousal of monetary union (Reich 1990:92).

During the electioneering of 1990, NF lost many members to other parties and groups, including a reportedly anti-socialist organization called Forum Partei, but a core of members continued on for a while in an effort to assist East Germans in dealing with the difficulties of the unification. New Forum has in recent years splintered into a number of new organizations (Torpey 1995).

Democracy Now

Democracy Now (*Demokratie Jetzt* or DJ) emerged out of the "Appeal for Interference in Our Own Affairs" published by twelve people on 12 September 1989. Signees of the statement included Ulrike Poppe (a former IFM member), Wolfgang Ullmann (a theology professor), and Konrad Weiss (a film director). The Appeal called for a coalition between Christians and critical Marxists to create a democratic socialist society in the GDR. According to Hamilton (1990:92), "although skeptical of German unity at first, by mid-December 1989 the group had announced a three-stage-plan for German unity, which included the call for a popular referendum on the question of the state unity of Germany after political reforms in the GDR. During the election campaign the movement called for a measured approach to German unity." Church historian Wolfgang Ullmann represented DJ at the round table discussions between the opposition movement and the GDR state between December 1989 and 1990 and served as Minister Without Portfolio in Hans Modrow's "government of national responsibility."

DJ reportedly has many base groups (*Basisgruppen*) throughout the new German states. A DJ representative told me that the organization is suspicious of political parties since they are monolithic entities that generally do not represent the constituencies that they claim to represent. Wolfgang Ullmann, one of the founding members of DJ, stated that political parties are "organizational forums from the last century. Now is the time of citizens' movements; creating political determination is no longer possible without a grass-roots democratic citizens' movement. And that is what we want to be" (*Berliner Zeitung*, December 24, 1989). The DJ representative told me that DJ advocates West German subsidization of the East Germany economic development and unemployed East

German workers. Konrad Weiss, a prominent DJ leader, supported the Israeli position on the Palestinian issue, a position that resulted in division within DJ (Buendnis 2000 1991:9).

Initiative for Peace and Human Rights (IFM)

Initiative for Peace and Human Rights (*Initiative fuer Frieden und Menschenrechte* or IFM) constituted the first opposition group in the GDR that deliberately positioned itself outside of the Evangelical church (Joppke 1995:101). An IFM representative told me that IFM, which was established in 1986, is the oldest independent peace group in East Germany. IFM attempted to ban West German political parties from participating in the GDR elections of March 1991. The group claimed to have some 200 members and has *Arbeitsgruppen* (work groups) that focus on draft resistance, victims of Stasi harassment, support for foreign workers, and women's issues. In recent years it has been discovered that eight out of the sixteen founding members of IFM were Stasi agents (Joppke 1995:xii).

Representatives from NF, DJ, and IFM belonging to Alliance 90 occasionally meet together. I attended one such "coordination meeting" in the House of Democracy on 26 February 1991. Eight males and one female ranging in age from their twenties to sixties, with a concentration of relatively young people, were present. Despite the fact that the opposition groups referred to gender equality as one of their goals, as Penrose observes, by and large they failed to include

> women's demands in their initial platforms, nor did any take
> a stand on other women's issues such as discriminatory
> employment practices, the closing of child care facilities, and
> the problems of single parents. Only the Vereinigte Linke
> approached women's groups - in November 1989 - with the
> offer to work together. Some reformers excused this lack of
> interest in women's policies with the argument that equality of
> the sexes had already been established in the GDR; others
> maintained that such problems did not have precedence at this
> time (Penrose 1993:39).

As a consequence, the Independent Women's Association (*Unabhaenige Frauden Verband* or UFV) has attempted to represent women's rights. It was established on 3 December 1989 by some 1,000 women. Although UFV achieved some visibility by its presence at the central Round Table in East Berlin and in the interim government of Hans Modrow in early 1990, it has evolved into a relatively marginalized women's group in the new Germany at a time when women's rights have come under considerable assault (Ferree and Young 1993; Marvin 1995). At any rate, the moderator proposed a discussion of the common goals of NF, DJ, and IFM. One representative spoke of the need for the constituent organizations to inform each other better about each other's events, perhaps by placing notices in the display window on the ground floor of the House of Democracy. Representatives also discussed the Gulf War and efforts to address the threat of rent increases in East Germany, including those of two tenants' associations in East Berlin. On 14 March 1992, I attended a Round Table from Below (*Runden Tisch von Unten*) which was attended by representatives of all three organizations affiliated with Alliance 90 but also representatives from the United Left, the Gray Panthers, and the student council at Humboldt University. The representatives debated whether the time was ripe to resume the Monday demonstrations that were so popular during the Wende, but this time directed at the Treuhand. One representative proposed the slogan, "The street is ours" ("*Unser ist die Strasse*") serve as the rallying cry for the demonstrations.

The Round Table that I attended was part of a new tradition that had developed in the GDR during the Wende. According to Marcuse, Round Tables were first convened locally on the initiative of New Forum and other citizens' groups, and organized on the national level in December 1989. "They were a coming together of all the oppositional forces, whether organized as political parties or as citizens' movements, sitting together with representatives of the old parties, chaired by competent and impartial church leaders. Originally views differed as to their precise role: some saw them as places where the opposition and the government would discuss/negotiate policy issues, others as super-parliaments. The national Round Table ended as virtually a second legislative body, passing proposals through to the "elected" parliament and effectively commenting on the proposals coming from the government on their way to parliament" (Marcuse 1991:19).

United Left

United Left (*Vereinigte Linke* or VL) is a loose grouping of anti-Stalinists who initially favored the creation of democratic socialism in the GDR. The group defines itself as part of the international and European left and accepts members from other grass-roots organizations and political parties. In the March 1990 election, VL formed a coalition with *die Nelken* (the Carnations) – a leftist group which seeks to integrate the writings of Marx, Engels, Lenin, and the German revolutionaries, Karl Liebknecht and Rosa Luxemburg (Hamilton 1990:40). At its headquarters in the Haus der Demokratie, VL displays a poster of Marx and also draws inspiration from the writings of Rosa Luxemburg - one of the Founders of the German Communist Party (KPD), a critic of Lenin's concept of democratic centralism, and a leftist martyr due to her assassination at the hands of the proto-Nazi *Freikorps*. Many opposition groups both prior to and during the Wende drew inspiration from the following passage from Luxemburg's 1917 essay titled "The Problem of Dictatorship," in which she critiqued the workings of Lenin's concept of "democratic centralism":

> Freedom only for the supporters of the government, only for members of one party - however numerous they may be - is no freedom at all. Freedom is always and exclusively freedom for the one who thinks differently. Not because of any fanatical concept of "justice" but because all that is instructive, wholesome and purifying in political freedom depends on this essential characteristic, and its effectiveness vanishes when "freedom" becomes a special privilege (quoted in Gleye 1991:73).

The following account of the history and objectives of VL is based largely upon a series of interviews that I had with Thomas Klein and Bernd Gehrke, the principal leaders (sometimes referred to as the "grandfathers" of the group since they were both in their early forties and somewhat older than most other members of the organization in early 1991). Klein wore a beard and slightly long hair which was balding in the rear, wore boots, and often carried a helmet because he rides a motorcycle to his various appointments. Klein was a former SED member who spent some time in a Stasi prison for his criticisms of the GDR state. In the last year of the GDR, he served as a democratically-elected member of the Volkskammer. Gehrke was expelled from SED in the 1970s and was one of the founders of the Green League (*Gruene Liga*), an organization which was formed by church-based environmentalists and members of the state ecology (*Staatekologie*) groups. He also held membership in New Forum. The opposition movement in the GDR consisted of two broad groupings: (1) the SED anti-Stalinists and (2) the citizens' movement (*Buergerbewegung*). Anti-Stalinist SED members were expelled from the party at various points in time, such as in 1968 for criticizing the Soviet invasion (which also involved GDR troops), in 1970, 1974, 1976, and in 1980 for supporting the Solidarity movement in Poland. The "leftists" in the SED had difficulty gathering as a unit due to suppression by the state and often lost their jobs and were arrested and imprisoned. In the fall of 1989 the opposition movement in the GDR became interested in obtaining legal status. In the process of doing so, its various tendencies formed separate organizations. In September 1989 various people proposed the establishment of an anti-Stalinist and anti-capitalist organization that would be part of the development of a democratic socialist society in the GDR. Some 200 individuals gathered at the (Environmental Library) in the *Zionskirche* in Prenzlauer Berg on 2 October 1989, in order to discuss the formation of such an organization. A small group of people established VL at a workshop on 24 and 25 November 1989.

VL is an "action alliance" consisting of "leftists" of different stripes rather than a political party per se. VL drew its members from the following groupings: (1) illegal groups within the SED, (2) illegal student and labor union groups, (3) people affiliated with the Umweltbibliothek, (4) young people who studied the writings of Trotsky, Buhakrin, Luxemburg, Havemann, and Bahro. Although the majority of the members in New Forum, Democracy Now, and Initiative for Peace and Human Rights (which are all members of Alliance 90) can be described as "radical democrats," "leftists" are present in them as well. Within the context of the new German states, VL defines itself as a link between the grass-roots groups, particularly Alliance 90 and the Independent Women's Association (which also reportedly exhibits leftist tendencies), and the Party of Democratic Socialism. In 1991 VL included within its ranks some New Forum members, PDS members, and Greens. VL maintains ties with leftists in Western Europe, particularly with the United Socialist Party in West Germany, as well as in the former Soviet Union and Eastern Europe. Although Klein and Gehrke define themselves as "revolutionary Marxists," some VL members are skeptical of Marxist analysis.

VL's immediate objective is not the construction of a democratic socialist society in Germany. Klein asserted that the concept of socialism first must be rejuvenated since it had been discredited by Stalinism. VL had little time to discuss theoretical issues during the Wende since it continually had to respond to new developments. Gehrke noted that both fascism and Stalinism historically fragmented alliances between leftist movements and working-class people. He added that East German workers tend to reject terms such "working class" and "socialism" and felt that Germany faced the danger of a resurgence of fascism, particularly if widespread disillusionment with the CDU occurs. Gehrke maintained that demonstrations in the wake of the unification pointed to the emergence of a new working-class movement in East Germany, but one that focuses on traditional trade union demands. He lamented that the grass-roots groups lacked any clear-cut programs for East German workers and lacked an economic alternative to capitalism. He maintained that the most members of the opposition movement are intellectuals and humanists who lack a feeling for problems of the East German masses. Gehrke said that VL is the only opposition group that has made some effort to develop an analysis of economic issues in the East German states. He said that some VL members were attempting to establish contacts with workers, but they constituted a minority of the group.

VL reportedly had some 200 members in East Berlin and several chapters in various other East German cities. A meeting of the Berlin chapter of VL that I attended on 20 February 1991 consisted of only one woman but ton males, ranging in age between their twenties and forties. The VL meeting that I attended the following day consisted of about 32 attendees from various parts of East Germany, only five or six of whom were females. The oldest people in attendance were men probably in their fifties. The representatives spent a considerable amount of time discussing the group's financial difficulties and the most appropriate uses of its resources, such as extra-parliamentary protest activities and support for squatters. One representative told me that debates within VL include whether it is further to the left than PDS and whether PDS is a social democratic or socialist organization. He lamented that the loose organization of VL prevents it from conducting more efficient meetings and that representatives often wandered in and out of meetings because they found them so boring.

The Party of Democratic Socialism as the Spurned Partner of the Opposition in the New German States

Whereas the Socialist Unity Party with the Politburo at its helm functioned as the ruling party in the GDR, its successor, the Party of Democratic Socialism (*Partei des Demokratischen Sozialismus* or PDS) has by default become part of the opposition in the new German states. The SED temporarily changed its name to SED-PDS before adopting its present name on 4 February 1990. PDS was led by a 100-member board of directors which was chaired by Gregor Gysi, a lawyer of Jewish background who defended the SED regime's most prominent opponents, including Rudolf Bahro, Robert Havemann, and Baerbel Bohley. Gysi unsuccessfully attempted to forge an alliance of the left at the time of the March 1990 election. Although PDS obtained only 16.33 percent of the votes in this election in the GDR as a whole, it received an impressive 30 percent of the vote in East Berlin whereas Alliance 90 received only 6.5 percent of the vote. Rossman argues that PDS remains a viable force in East German politics:

> Ironically, it is the PDS which has reaped the fruits of the opposition's self-marginalization and the SPD's wholesale adaptation to the exigencies of West German electoral politics. On the verge of self-dissolution earlier this year, the PDS has staged one of the most remarkable comebacks in recent history. Under the brilliant leadership of Gregor Gysi, the party has effectively chucked out the majority of the old guard, divested itself of much of its property, and succeeded, through the co-optation of many of the opposition's slogans and demands, in projecting the image of a "modern socialist party" defending the interests of workers, women, and the environment. . . . Reconciled to the loss of power, the PDS accomplished its more modest goal of becoming a strong opposition force (Rossman 1990:72).

Gysi favors efforts to democratize PDS even further and accepts the party's role as an oppositional force in the new Germany. He favors forming the creation of alliances between PDS and the citizen groups and would like to see PDS evolve into an all-German party that clearly provides a clear democratic socialist alternative to the SPD (Runge and Stelbrink 1990).

Most members of the grass-roots groups that emerged during the Wende regard PDS as a pariah organization that has yet to prove its trustworthiness. Although Alliance 90 and its constituent bodies tend to keep PDS at a distance, VL and the Independent Women's Association serve in part as bridges between the two. Like many East Germans, members of the grass-roots organizations wonder to what extent PDS can shed its SED legacy and even purge itself of Stalinist elements. In this section, I present observations obtained in interviews with two scholars who studied the transition from the SED to the PDS during the early 1990s.

Dr. Heinrich Bordtfeldt's Observations on PDS

Heinrich Bortfeldt is a former SED member who earned his Ph.D. in English and history from Martin Luther University and his DSc in history from Humboldt University. He joined the SED at age 27 and worked for the Academy for Societal Studies (*Akademie fuer Gesellschaftliches Studium*), an affiliate of the Central Committee (ZK) which conducted social scientific and historical research for the Politburo and the ZK. The Rektor of the Academy served as a member of the ZK. Bortfeldt spent three months in 1988 as a visiting scholar at Stanford University and completed his dissertation B in 1989 on studies of the GDR conducted by American scholars. Bortfeldt spent the 1991-1992 academic year on a German Marshall Fund research fellowship at Virginia Military Institute and Stanford University, but was unable to obtain a position in the history department at Humboldt University. According to Fisher (1995:189), "he managed by 1994 to create some semblance of a livelihood by teaching police recruits in Brandenburg, writing occasionally for western journals, and leading an occasional seminar at the Free University" in West Berlin.

In 1990 he authored a pamphlet titled *Von der SED zur PDS - Aufbruch zu neuen Ufern?* (From SED to PDS - Departure to New Shores?) which was published by the Commission of Political Education of the Board of Directors of the PDS (Bortfeldt 1990). The pamphlet discusses the transformation of SED into PDS that occurred between the summer of 1989 and March 18, 1990 - the date of the first democratic election in GDR history. Bortfeldt also has written a manuscript based upon his interviews with former SED and PDS leaders, including Egon Krenz and Hans Modrow. He resigned his membership in PDS after the expose of the party's transfer of funds to the Soviet Union in order to avoid possible appropriation of these funds by the FRG government.

Bortfeldt stated that although most SED members were dissatisfied with social conditions within the party and in the GDR, rank-and-file members were completely powerless due to the SED's rigid centralism under which they were to treat the leadership's statements as holy. The Party Control Commission served as a deterrent against dissent within the SED and expulsion from the SED resulted in marginalization in GDR society. Bortfeldt maintained that the SED elites lived like feudal lords, although he noted that Honecker himself rode in a modest French Citroen and retained some semblance of proletarianism. He asserted that Honecker defined socialism in terms of access to certain basic material items, such as food and shelter, but seemed unaware that the material desires of the masses, which included access to quality goods and a desire to travel to the West, had changed since the emergence of the GDR. Bortfeldt suspected that Honecker was partly senile, evidenced in part by his failure to express regrets for his actions, except for his decision not to retire in 1987, in extensive interviews published in a book titled *Der Sturz* (*The Fall*) (Andert and Herzberg 1990). Initially many SED members felt enthusiastic about perestroika in the Soviet Union, but more and more of them became irritated by the ongoing economic difficulties there. Bortfeldt maintained that the Politburo had access to several sources of information concerning the mood of the GDR masses, including reports (which emphasized primarily unity and achievements but also mentioned problems) from the party Bezirk secretaries, Stasi reports, and over 50,000 letters, most of which were filled with complaints, but chose to ignore or deny the existence of extensive dissatisfaction in the country.

Borfeldt described PDS as a very different party than the SED was. Whereas the SED had 2,324,995 members in 1988, the PDS had 350,491 members in June 1990 (Bortfeldt 1990). In March 1991 Bortfeldt stated that the number of PDS had fallen to some 250,000. The leadership of PDS is basically reform-oriented. Whereas the Politburo members never joked about themselves or the SED, Gysi is young, intelligent, witty, and has a good sense of humor. In contrast to the SED party groups which were situated primarily in work sites, the PDS has its party groups primarily in residential areas. The PDS also lacks combat groups (*Kampfgruppen*) that the SED had, but has organized some of its younger members into working groups.

Bortfeldt identified three main streams within the PDS: (1) the democratic socialists, such as Gysi, who favor political action, assistance for the unemployed, and oppose both a dogmatic brand of Marxism-Leninism and social democracy; (2) the Marxist-Leninists whose ranks include many young "revolutionary Marxists" and many hard-liners left over from the SED; and (3) the social democrats who believe that socialism is out of the question for a long period of time and thus stress efforts to humanize capitalism. He said that 47 percent of PDS members are pensioners, probably most of whom are Leninist hard-liners who have acted as an obstruction in efforts to reform PDS. About 8 to 9 percent of PDS members are under 30 years of age. Bortfeldt noted that many teachers, civil servants, and intellectuals had left the PDS because they had been instructed to fill out forms at their place of employment that asked if they were members of a Communist party. Only about 10 percent of PDS members are workers because most of them left the SED during the first phase of the Wende in October - November 1989. According to Bortfeldt, PDS has been attempting to establish contacts with other left of center political parties and groups. PDS has been involved in some 100 official dialogues with the SPD as well as many unofficial ones. Some Greens and left-wing SPD members conducted discussions with PDS but ceased their contacts after the PDS financial scandal. PDS has about 1,000 members in West Germany. Bortfeldt noted that PDS groups in West Germany have been infiltrated by the German Communist Party (DKP), a discredited organization because it received funding from the SED. He maintained that PDS for the most part is an isolated body which has no significant influence in the new Germany. PDS is even more marginalized from the life of East German workers than was the SED.

Bortfeldt noted that East German intellectuals and PDS leaders were surprised by the conservative victory in the March 1990 election because they anticipated that the SPD and the PDS would emerge as the dominant parties in East Germany. He asserted that most East Germans are not intellectuals and felt material deprivation relative to West Germans. When a team of Academy researchers visited a glass blowing factory near Erfurt, the principal desires listed by the workers were a sufficient supply of materials in order to work without interruptions, good wages for hard work, and availability of consumer goods. The workers did not mention concepts such democracy, socialism, or capitalism. Such notions were the concern primarily of intellectuals, who, according to Bortfeldt, failed to grasp the mood of GDR workers. The ZK commissioned an analysis of some 800 letters protesting the ban on *Sputnik* in October 1988, most of which were sent by intellectuals as opposed to workers or peasants; Bortfeldt noted the rift between intellectuals and workers had widened over time in the GDR. As a consequence, East German intellectuals tended to maintain an arrogant attitude toward workers and felt disillusioned by their preference for unification over the opportunity to create a democratic socialist society in the GDR. Bortfeldt maintained that the concept of socialism will remain discredited among the East German masses for some time to come.

Dr. Frank Adler's Observations on PDS

Frank Adler, DSc, is the business leader (*Geschaeftsfuehrer*) of the *Berliner Instituet fuer Sozialwissenschaftliche Studien* (Berlin Institute for Social Scientific Studies). Although the Institute formerly was an affiliate of the Central Committee, it is not a nonprofit corporation. The Institute has project groups focusing on the following aspects of the unification in East Germany: (1) the "winners" and the "losers" in the unification process; (2) small firms and independent entrepreneurs, and (3) microscopic issues, such as antagonism toward foreigners, East German identity, and changes in value orientations. The Institute is also conducting research on the SED-PDS transition, changes in political socialization in East Germany, and political developments in Germany and other European countries.

Dr. Adler stated that the SED acted as a power elite with tremendous control in a system of "actually existing socialism." He argued that while the GDR was not a socialist society in ideal terms, it also was not a capitalist society. As for the question as to whether the Stasi constituted a "state within a state" or a "state behind a state," Adler maintained the SED had ultimate control over the Stasi, although he did admit that the Stasi had managed to obtain a certain degree of autonomy in the last years of the GDR. He asserted that there are many exaggerated tales about the power of the Stasi. In his opinion, the Stasi was not an omnipresent threat to the general population but played this role for opposition groups within the churches and for those East Germans who sought exile. Adler felt that the Stasi has become a scapegoat for many of the problems in East Germany. Conversely, he noted that the majority of SED members exhibited little civic courage and went along with the status quo, although most of them don't want to take responsibility for their actions.

Adler said that PDS is the only East German party that can mobilize 10,000 people for a demonstration, but has become an isolated and stigmatized body with deep internal divisions. He identified three streams within PDS: 1) the young reformers, (2) the Western leftists of different tendencies, and (3) the "old-timers" which make about a third of the membership. Adler believes that DKP may allow itself to be absorbed by PDS, a move which may drive some PDS members into the SPD. He noted that a looming question is whether or not PDS can lose its pariah status if it is able to develop attractive social programs for East Germany. Adler noted that it is difficult to predict the future of East Germany. He stated that the unification resembles a process of colonization in some ways, adding that the distinction between the West and East in Germany resembles that between the North and the South in Italy. Adler suggested that social equilibrium of some sort may not be achieved in East Germany for ten to fifteen years. He doesn't believe that market mechanisms will be sufficient to achieve parity between the West and East, but that state subsidies will be needed for this to occur. Adler maintained that "actually existing socialism" does not have a viable future and that no meaningful institutional alternative to capitalism exists at the present time.

Prospects for PDS

Although still regarded with much suspicion by both East Germans and members of the various grass-roots groups, PDS functions as a part of the new opposition in the new German states. Like the smaller opposition, groups, PDS has found its greatest appeal among East German intellectuals. Gysi, who stepped down as PDS chairperson in February 1993, calls for a "third way" in the new Germany - one that emphasizes "radical democracy, constitutional state humanism, social justice, protection of the environment, establishment of true emancipation and equality for women" (Woods 1993:59). In July 1992, Gysi, along with Peter-Michael Diestel (a member of the Christian Democratic Union and the former interior minister in the last of the GDR), became a key-figure in the creation of the Committee for Justice - an effort to address the socioeconomic crisis faced by many East Germans in the wake of the unification. While various elements within PDS also supported this new "East German movement," the party did not give its undivided support to it (*Der Spiegel*, No. 30, 1992, p. 21). Gysi stepped down as PDS chairperson in February 1993 and was replaced by Lothar Bilsky. He referred to PDS "as a socialist party furthest to the left from social democracy" (*Deutsches Nachtrichten*, February 5, 1993, p. 2).

Only time will tell whether PDS will emerge as a significant voice of the East German masses or whether it will wither away as a relic of the former GDR. By 1994 its membership had declined drastically to some 173,000 (Brie 1995:36). In terms of age composition, a recent survey revealed that 37 percent of its members are over 65 years of age, 33 percent are between 55 and 64, 22 percent are between 35 and 54, and only 7 percent are 34 or younger (Wittich 1995:67). This differs drastically from the age composition of Alliance 90/Greens in which only 5 percent of the members are over age 65, 8 percent are between 55 and 64, 61 percent are between 35 and 54, and 27 percent are 34 or younger. In contrast, as Canepa observes, however, these figures are somewhat misleading:

> [T]he looseness of party structure, the ability of non-members to be active in it. . . and the blacklisting that attends PDS membership all tend to reduce the incentive to acquire official membership. There are significant numbers of young PDS activists who have never requested membership (Canepa 1994:323).

Whether PDS will gain the confidence of East Germans depends in large part upon its ability not only to address their new status as second-class citizens within the new Germany but also its willingness to come to terms with its Stalinist past. In reality PDS wishes to obtain a foothold in the old German states, but its success thus far there has been quite limited. At the annual party conference on 27 through 29 January, 1995, Gysi proposed that the next conference be held in the West German city of Bremen (*Deutschland Nachtrichten*, 3 February 1995). Despite such efforts, by and large PDS constitutes at the present time a regional protest party. It has what some perceive to have become the leading actor in the East German tenants' movement (Canepa 1994:333).

PDS has 30 representatives in the Bundestag and some 6,000 representatives at various levels of government in the new German states (Brie 1995:11). This latter figure includes 161 mayors, four of whom preside over the municipal governments of four large cities, and 26 representatives in the city council in East Berlin. PDS presently constitutes the third largest party in the new German states and obtained 4.4 percent of the votes in the whole of Germany in the Bundestag election of 1994. Although PDS faces numerous struggles to ensure its permanence in Germany Canepa (1994:337) asserts that "PDS has weathered the storms thus far, defying earlier predictions of its imminent demise, and has by now politically turned a decisive corner." At a time when the *Realos* have come to dominate the Green Party and formed a coalition with the SPD in North Rhineland-West Phalia, it appears that PDS offers the clearest leftist alternative in not only the new German states but also the old German states.

Chapter 8

Lessons from the Short History of the German Democratic Republic

In this concluding chapter, I adopt a reflexive approach in assessing the 40-year history of the German Democratic Republic, not only its shortcomings but also its achievements. The collapse of the GDR must be viewed within the larger context of the demise of neo-Stalinism in the Soviet Union and Eastern Europe. Did the collapse of the GDR serve as one more example that capitalism is the end of history or may it provide the space by which democratic socialist ideals eventually may blossom as East Germans come to grips with the realities of their second-class citizenship in the new Germany?

Many, if not most, East Germans regarded the GDR as a socialist society because the means of production had been nationalized, but also as an imperfect form of socialism which needed to undergo a process of democratization. While pockets of reform-oriented people functioned within the SED, the centralized bureaucratic structure of the party did not allow them to have much impact. Many rank-and-file SED members admitted that the GDR manifested many contradictions related to external and internal factors that had shaped its historical development. The most visible effort to democratize the GDR took the form of peace, environmental, and human rights groups which found sanctuary within the Evangelical church. West German leftists often rather naively viewed the GDR in utopian terms and hoped that it would evolve into a more humane Germany. Peter Schneider (1991:66-91), a prominent West Berlin novelist and social commentator, faulted his fellow West German leftists for having overlooked the contradictory nature of the GDR.

Many East Germans, particularly reform-oriented SED members and members of the citizens' movements, held out the hope during the Wende that a democratic socialist GDR could finally be developed. According to Glaessner,

> Despite decades of disappointment, hope for an alternative to capitalism was stronger in the GDR than in other socialist countries. The collapse of 'real socialism' again nurtured the hope that this goal could now at last be reached (Glaessner 1992:118).

The West German weekly *Quick* conducted a poll which indicated 67 percent of East Germans favored "socialism with a human face" while only 33 percent favored adoption of the West German social market economy (Le Gloannec 1991:60-61).

Peter Marcuse (1991:266-275) lists the following "key characteristics" of the GDR: (1) material scarcity compared to the FRG and other Western societies; (2) a repressive Stalinist state; (3) centralized economic planning; (4) an anti-market ideology; (5) the priority of the workplace; (6) a merger of economic and social goals; (7) a class structure which privileged high-echelon party and state functionaries, artists and cultural leaders, and outstanding athletes; (8) and a "stated commitment to egalitarianism and social justice." As this listing indicates, the GDR was a contradictory society - one which represented major discrepancies between the ideals and the realities of socialism. Nevertheless, despite the persistence of social inequality in the GDR, it had managed to narrow the socioeconomic gap between those at the highest echelons and those at the lowest echelons of the society more than is the case in capitalist societies. Gleye (1991:197), who explicitly identifies himself as a non-Marxist, notes that "I had to conclude that the Marxist visionaries of East Germany had achieved a substantial degree of success in organizing their society, a society that clashed to the core with the economic foundation of Western society by removing wealth as the basis for social differentiation and access to the things that society had to offer."

My own observations also indicated that on the whole East Germans had internalized egalitarian ideals much more than people in capitalist societies where discrepancies in income and wealth are widely accepted as part and parcel of the supposedly natural order of things. In part based upon my first-hand experiences in the GDR and conversations with a cross-section of its people and the observations of others, I tend to view the GDR, the Soviet Union, and other East European societies as having constituted transitory social formations between capitalism and socialism since they were established on the basis of socialist ideals and continued, at least in theory, to be guided by them - despite their bureaucratization, hierarchical relations, lack of certain democratic processes, and contradictory governmental practices on various issues.

Ironically, as Gouldner (1976:292) notes, "socialist ideology fosters expectations and tensions subversive of those structures of domination characteristic of 'socialist' nations today." Many GDR citizens had learned the ideals of socialism, often had internalized them, but realized that their society fell far short of these ideals. Despite its success in propagating a "vision of a society of relative equality" (Glaessner 1992:122) at the socioeconomic level, the SED elite monopolized political power - a practice that violated the principles of economic democracy. As Marcuse observes,

> Creativity, innovation, self-expression, have been absent from most of DDR production (the creative arts, drama, are a conspicuous exception); very few workers would say their jobs have contributed to the free unfolding of their personalities. Nor has democratic, self-determination ever characterized work processes in the DDR, despite official propaganda to the contrary (Marcuse 1991:279-280).

The German Democratic Republic is a social formation of the past which has been united with, or, more accurately stated, has been absorbed by the Federal Republic of Germany under the sponsorship of the CDU. As Rosenberg (1991:250) argues, "Instead of finding themselves accepted as equally empowered citizens within a federal republic, the East Germans are experiencing a class colonization process under which the rights of the natives are by definition inferior to the colonizer." Many West Germans and East Germans disparagingly refer to each other as *Wessis* and *Ossis*, respectively. West Germans often accuse East Germans of being *faul* (lazy) and assert that they have to learn how to work hard before they share fully in the benefits of the social market economy or welfare capitalism. East Germans often retort that the West Germans are *arrogant* and self-centered and maintain that, despite its defects, not everything was Mist (dung) in the GDR. If one views ethnicity as a dynamic process of cultural identity, one might posit the argument that while East Germans and West Germans no longer constitute separate German nationality groups, they may be evolving into two separate ethnic groups within the same nation-state.

Indeed, Howard (1995:48) contends that "East and West German identities are becoming polarized." In his view, although East Germans do not distinguish themselves from West Germans by race, language, or religion, they constitute an ethnic group within the new Germany because "they are to a large extent self-perpetuating and territorially bounded; they have powerful and emotional ties to a common past, common values, common struggles; they are represented politically and are opposed to a common 'other'" (Howard 1995:56). Elisabeth Noelle-Neumann of the Allesbach Institute has documented a growing Ossi-Wessi split based upon response to the question: "Do you agree that 'we are one people'?" Whereas she found that in 1990 54 percent of West Germans and 45 percent of East Germans agreed with the statement, she found that in 1994 47 percent of West Germans and only 28 percent of East Germans agreed with it (Schoenbaum and Pond 1996:3). In the wake of the unification, Schneider (1991:17) suggests that a new pattern of ethnic stratification appears to be emerging in West Berlin, where the "arrivals will undoubtedly develop a very clear pecking order, with the East Germans at the top of the ladder, the ethnic Germans from Poland, Hungary, Romania, and the Soviet Union down below, and the "non-German" foreigners on the very bottom rung."

The Bundestag responded to social unrest in the new German states by increasing subsidies for social welfare and construction there. Nevertheless, West German corporations on the whole continue to be cautious about investing in the East. Despite Koehl's promises to East Germans that their socioeconomic situation would improve, major economic disparities will exist between West and East Germany for some time to come, in much the same way that regional differences exist in other advanced capitalist countries, including Italy and the United States. Whereas Germany's political capital is in the process of moving from Bonn to Berlin, the financial capital will be concentrated in the West for some time to come. As Torpey (1995:128) observes, "the eastern German's initial euphoria over unification has subsided in large measure because so many of them view themselves as having been cheated by the powers-that-be, who promised so much and delivered so little." A poll conducted by the West German news magazine *Der Spiegel* (1995) reported that 72 percent of East Germans viewed themselves as second-class citizens in 1995 and 68 percent felt that the FRG state does not do enough to improve the living conditions in the new German states.

As East Germans learn first-hand the realities of capitalism, many of them appear to be revisiting the ideals of socialism to which they were exposed. What lessons may we draw from the GDR experience as to the prospects for constructing a socialist world system, one that incorporates the redistributive features of existing socialist-oriented or post-revolutionary societies but discards their authoritarian and productivist features? The GDR experience suggests that the construction of democratic socialism will be a long, protracted, and multilinear process (and by no means an inevitable one) and provides yet another reminder that socialism cannot be built in one country.

The contradictions of post-revolutionary societies, including the GDR, have been shaped by both internal and external forces. Marx and Engels argued that socialism has to emerge within capitalist societies with highly developed productive forces. Sherman and Wood (1979:261) maintain that "political dictatorship in the Soviet Union resulted from the Russian autocratic tradition, the underground political tradition, civil war, foreign wars (and encirclement), and from economic backwardness." Despite the fact that it achieved a higher level of economic development than the Soviet Union ever did, the GDR inherited many of the liabilities of its parent society.

While the unification of Germany is a reality that is here to stay, both East and West Germans need to consider the development of a "third way" that recognizes two issues: (1) the achievements of the GDR, despite its many glaring contradictions, in achieving a more equitable social system than has historically existed in capitalist societies, even in Western Europe, and (2) the vision that many members of the East German opposition had developed in an embryonic form. Ironically, progressive elements within the PDS exhibit perhaps the clearest vision of a "third way" in the new Germany. Although still regarded with suspicion by both East Germans and members of the various grass-roots groups, PDS functions as a significant force in the new opposition in East Germany. According to Braunthal,

> The PDS program - reflecting an eclectic mix of communist, green, social democratic, feminist, and radical democratic elements - calls for a fundamental transformation of society and democratization of the economy, which would eventually lead to a democratic socialism. The program rejects dictatorship and the use of force. It no longer claims that the party is the sole representative of the Left but rather the center of different leftist streams. Thus the PDS sees itself as a

movement that would be open to the Greens, left-wing SPD members, and independents (Braunthal 1995:44-45).

According to Gysi (1995:140), "the PDS is positioning itself as a modern democratic and socialist party convinced of the need to transcend social relations dominated by capital."

Over the long run, developments in East Germany depend in large part upon developments in the capitalist world-system, which continues to exhibit numerous contradictions, despite the common belief that the collapse of Stalinism and the Soviet empire constituted the "end of history." Political tendencies, such as the Greens and progressive forces in PDS, may eventually pave the way for the construction of a more communal, egalitarian and humanitarian model of the just society than capitalism can ever promise. Ultimately, however, such a project will have to be part and parcel of the construction of socialism on a worldwide scale. The collapse of Bolshevikism, not only in the Soviet Union but also Eastern Europe, and the ongoing contradictions of the capitalist world-system that contribute to a growing gap between rich and poor and a pillaging of the environment hold out, as Chomsky (1990:133) suggests, "prospects for the revival of libertarian socialist and radical democratic ideals that had languished, including popular control of the workplace and investment decisions, and, correspondingly, the entrenchment of political democracy as constraints imposed by private power are reduced."

References

Andert, Reinhold, and Wolfgang Herzberg. 1990. *Der Sturz: Erich Honecker im Kreuzverhoer*. Berlin and Weimar: Aufbau-Verlag.

Ardagh, John. 1987. *Germany and the Germans: An Anatomy of Society Today*. New York: Harper & Row.

Aronowitz, Stanley. 1990. A New Stage of History. *New Politics* 2(4):5-11.

Baer, Hans A. 1984. *The Black Spiritual Movement: A Religious Response to Racism*. Knoxville: University of Tennessee Press.

Baer, Hans A. 1988. *Recreating Utopia in the Desert: A Sectarian Response to Modern Mormonism*. Albany: State University of New York Press.

Baer, Hans A., and Merrill Singer. 1992. *African-American in the Twentieth Century: Varieties of Protest and Accommodation*. Knoxville: University of Tennessee Press.

Bahro, Rudolf. 1978. *The Alternative in Eastern Europe*. London: Verso.

Barnett, Thomas P. 1992. *Romanian and East German Policies in the Third World: Comparing the Strategies of Ceasescu and Honecker*. Westport, CT: Praeger.

Baylis, Thomas A. 1974. *The Technical Intelligentsia and the East German Elite: Legitimacy and Social Change in Mature Communism*. Berkeley: University of California Press.

Borneman, John. 1991. *After the Wall: East Meets West in the New Berlin*. New York: Basic Books.

_____. 1992. *Belonging in the Two Berlins: Kin, State, Nation*. Cambridge: Cambridge University Press.

Bortfeldt, Heinrich. 1990. *Von der SED zur PDS - Aufbruch zu Neuen Ufern? Sommer/Herbst 1989 - 18 Maerz 1990*. Berlin: Kommission Bildung des Parteivorstandes der PDS.

Braunthal, Gerald. 1995. The Perspective for the Left. *German Politics and Society* 13(1):36-61.

Brie, Michael. 1995. Das polistiche Projekt PDS -- eine unmoegliche Moeglichkeit. In *Die PDS: Empirische Befunde & Kontroverse Analysen*. Michael Brie, Martin Herzig, and Thomas Koch, eds. Pp. 9-38. Koeln: PapaRosa Verlag.

Bronner, Stephen. 1994. *Of Critical Theory and Its Theorists*. Oxford: Blackwell.

Buendnis 2000. 1991. DJ-Mitglied bleiben oder nicht bleiben?

Buendnis 2000: Forum fuer Demokratie, Oekologie und Menschenrechte. No. 5, February 8, p. 9.

Burrant, Stephen R. 1988. The Society and Its Environment. In *East Germany: A Country Study*. Stephen R. Burrant, ed. Pp. 61-115. Washington, D.C.: U.S. Government Printing Office.

Canepa, Eric. 1994. Germany's Party of Democratic Socialism. In *Between Globalism and Nationalism: Socialist Register 1994*. Ralph Miliband and Leo Panitch, eds. Pp. 312-341. London: Merlin Press.

Chase-Dunn, C.K. 1982. Socialist States in the Capitalist World-Economy. In *Socialist States in the World-System*. C.K. Chase-Dunn, ed. Pp. 21-55. Beverly Hills, California: Sage.

Childs, David. 1983. *The GDR: Moscow's German Ally*. London: George Allen & Unwin.

Chomsky, Noam. 1990 The Dawn, So Far, Is the East. *The Nation*, January 29.

Clawson, P.J., et al. 1981. Introduction to a Special Issue on the Soviet Union. *Review of Radical Political Economics* 13(1):iii-viii.

Cole, John W. 1985. Problems of Socialism in Eastern Europe. *Dialectical Anthropology* 9:240.

Dennis, Mike. 1988. *German Democratic Republic: Politics, Economics and Society*. London and New York: Pinter.

Doud, David Tieman. 1995. *Berlin 2000: The Center of Europe*. Lanham, MD: University Press of America.

Dwyer, Kevin. 1979. The Dialog of Ethnology. *Dialectical Anthropology* 3:208-210.

Ehrenberg, John. 1992. *The Dictatorship of the Proletariat: Marxism's Theory of Socialist Democracy*. New York: Routledge.

Ferree, Myra Marx and Brigette Young. 1993. Three Steps Back for Women: German Unification, Gender, and University "Reform." *Political Science & Politics* 26(2):199-205.

Fisher, Marc. 1995. *After the Wall: Germany, the Germans and the Burdens of History*. New York: Simon & Schuster.

Foster, John Bellamy. 1994. *The Vulnerable Planet: A Short Economic History of the Environment*. New York: Monthly Review Press.

Frank, Andre Gunder. 1990. Revolution in Eastern Europe: Lessons for Democratic Socialist Movements (and Socialists). In *The Future of Socialism: Perspectives from the Left*. William K. Tabb, ed. Pp. 87-105. New York: Monthly Review Press.

Gates, Becky A. 1988. The Economy. In *East Germany: A Country Study*. Stephen R. Burrant, ed. Pp. 119-159. Washington, D.C.: U.S. Government Printing Office.

Glaessner, Gert Joachim. 1992. *The Unification Process in Germany: From Dictatorship to Democracy.* New York: St. Martin's Press.

Gleye, Paul. 1991. *Behind the Wall: An American in East Germany, 1988-1989.* Carbondale: Southern Illinois Press.

Goldman Marshall I. 1987. *Gorbachev's Challenge: Economic Reform in the Age of High Technology.* New York: W.W. Norton & Co.

Gouldner, Alvin. 1976. *The Dialectic of Ideology and Technology: The Origins, Grammar, and Future of Ideology.* New York: Seabury Press.

Gysi, Gregor. 1995. Five years of the PDS. *New Politics* 5(3):135-142.

Habermas, Juergen. 1975. *Legitimation Crisis.* Boston: Beacon Press.

_____. 1994. *The Past as Future.* Lincoln: University of Nebraska Press.

Haendel, Wolfgang. 1991. Switching Systems in Eastern Germany. In *Meet United Germany.* Susan Stern, ed. Pp. 100-109. Frankfurt am Main: Frankfurter Allegemeine Zeitung GmbH.

Hamilton, Daniel. 1990. *After the Revolution: The New Political Landscape in East Germany.* Washington, DC: American Institute for Contemporary German Studies.

Havemann, Robert. 1972. *Questions Answers Questions: From the Biography of a German Marxist.* New York: Doubleday.

Hermann, Detlef. 1984. Life Inside the SED. In *East Germany: A New German Nation Under Socialism?* Arthur McCardle and A. Bruce Boneau, eds. Pp. 127-135. Lanham, MD: University Press of America.

Howard, Marc. 1995. An East German Ethnicity?: Understanding the New Division of Unified Germany. *German Politics and Society* 13(4):49-68.

Joppke, Christian. 1995. *East German Dissidents and the Revolution of 1989: Social Movement in a Leninist Regime.* New York: New York University Press.

Juenger, Juergen, Werner Maiwald, and Siegfried Stoetzer. 1990. Economic Reform in the GDR. *Eastern European Economics* 29(1):30-40.

Kagarlitsky, Boris. 1990. *The Dialectic of Change.* London: Verso.

Kaiser, Karl. 1991. Foreign Policy Directions. In *Meet United Germany.* Susan Stern, ed. Pp. 145-151. Frankfurt: Frankfurter Allegemeine Zeitung GmbH.

Koelble, Thomas. 1991. After the Deluge: Unification and the Political Parties in Germany. *German Politics & Society,* Issue 22:45-59.

Krisch, Henry. 1985. *The German Democratic Republic: The Search for Identity.* Boulder, CO; Westview Press.

Laquer, Walter. 1985. *Germany Today: A Personal Report.* Boston: Little, Brown & Co.

Le Gloannec, Anne-Marie. 1991. Like Fire and Water? Two Germanies in One. In *German Unification in European Perspective.* Wolfgang Heisenberg, ed. Pp. 57-69. London: Brassey's.

Leonhard, Wolfgang. 1958. *Child of the Revolution.* Chicago: Henry Regnery.

Lippmann, Heinz. 1972. *Honecker and the New Politics of Europe.* New York: MacMillan.

Long, Tom. 1981. On The Nature of Soviet-type Societies: Two Perspectives from Eastern Europe. *Berkeley Journal of Sociology* 26:157-188.

Ludz, Peter. 1970. *The German Democratic Republic From the Sixties to the Seventies.* Cambridge, MA: Harvard Center for International Affairs.

_____. 1972. *The Changing Party Elite in East Germany.* Cambridge, MA: MIT Press.

Luft, Christa. 1990. Economic Reform in the GDR -- Concerns and Focal Points. *Eastern European Economics* 29(1):41-54.

Marcuse, Peter. 1990a. *A German Way of Revolution· DDR-Tagesbuch eines Amerikaners.* Berlin: Dietz Verlag.

_____. 1990b. Letter from the German Democratic Republic. *Monthly Review* 42(3):30-62.

_____. 1991. *Missing Marx: A Personal and Political Journal of a Year in East Germany, 1989-1990.* New York: Monthly Review Press.

Markus, G. 1982. Western Marxism and Eastern European Socialist. *Dialectical Anthropology* 6:291-318.

Marsh, David. 1991. The Aftermath of Unity. In *Meet United Germany.* Susan Stern, ed. Pp. 31-40. Frankfurt am Main: Frankfurter Allegemeine Zeitung GmbH.

Marvin, Grace M. 1995. Two Steps Back and One Step Forward: East German Women Since the Fall of the Wall. *Humanity and Society* 19(2):37- 52.

McAdams, A. James. 1985. *East Germany and Detente: Building Authority After the Wall.* Cambridge: Cambridge University Press.

_____. 1989. The GDR at Forty: The Perils of Success. *German Politics and Society.* No. 17:15-26.

McCauley, Martin. 1979. *Marxism-Leninism in the German Democratic Republic: The Socialist Unity Party (SED)*. New York: Barnes & Noble.

_____. 1983. *The German Democratic Republic Since 1945*. London: MacMillan Press Ltd.

Merkl, Peter H. 1993. *German Unification in the European Context*. University Park: Pennsylvania State University.

Meuschel, Sigrid. 1990. The End of "East German Socialism." *Telos*. No. 82:3-26.

Minnerup, Gunter. 1982. East Germany's Frozen Revolution. *New Left Review*, No. 132:5-32.

_____.1984. The GDR and the German Question in the 1980s. *GDR Monitor*. No. 4:3-13.

_____. 1989a. The October Revolution in East Germany. *Labour Focus on Eastern Europe*. No. 3:5-9.

_____. 1989b. Dawn of the Post-Wall Era. *Labour Focus on Eastern Europe*. No 3:3-4.

_____. 1990. Kohl Hijacks East German Revolution. *Labour Focus on Eastern Europe*. No. 1:4-7.

Naimark, Norman M. 1989. Forty Years After: The Origins of the GDR. *German Politics and Society*. Issue 17:1-13.

Navarro, Vincente. 1982. The Limits of the World Systems Theory in Defining Capitalist and Socialist Formations. *Science and Society* 46:77-90.

Panorama DDR. 1986. *The German Democratic Republic*. Berlin, GDR: Panorama.

Parsons, John E. 1989. Plan and Market in the Marxist Imagination: The Changing of the Guard among GDR Economists. *German Politics and Society*. No. 17:39-49.

Penrose, Virginia. 1993. The Political Participation of GDR Women during the Wende. In *Studies in GDR Culture and Society 11/12: The End of the GDR and the Problems of Integration*. Margy Gerber and Roger Woods, eds. Pp. 37-52. Lanham, MD: University Press of America.

Phillips, Ann L. 1986. *Soviet Policy Toward East Germany Reconsidered*. Westport, CT: Greenwood Press.

Pulzer, Peter. 1991. Political Parties and Democracy. In *Meet United Germany*. Susan Stern, ed. Pp. 52-67. Frankfurt am Main: Frankfurter Allgemeine Zeitung GmbH.

Radcliffe, Stanley. 1972. *25 Years on the Two Germanies, 1970*. London: Harrap.

Reich, Jens. 1990. Reflections on Becoming an East German Dissident, On Losing the Wall and a Country. In *Spring in Winter: The 1989 Revolutions*. Gwyn Prins, ed. Pp. 65-97. Manchester: Manchester University Press.

Rosenberg, Dorothy. 1991. The Colonization of East Germany. *Monthly Review* 43(2):14-33.

Rossman, Peter. 1990. The Paradox of the East German Revolution. *New Politics* 3:65-73.

Runge, Irene, and Uwe Stelbrink. 1990. *Gregor Gysi: "Ich bin Opposition"*. Berlin: Dietz Verlag.

Sandford, John. 1993. The Opposition on the Eve of the Revolution. In *Studies in GDR Culture and Society, Vols. 11/12*. Margy Gerber and Roger, eds. Pp. 19-36. Lanham, MD: University Press of America.

Scharf, C. Bradley. 1984. *Politics and Change in East Germany: The Evolution of Socialist Democracy*. Boulder, CO: Westview Press.

Schlommer, Friedrich

Schneider, Peter. 1991. *The German Comedy: Scenes of Life After the Wall*. New York: Farrar, Straus, Giroux.

Schnitzer, Martin. 1972. *East and West Germany: A Comparative Economic Analysis*. New York: Praeger.

Schoenbaum, David and Elizabeth Pond. 1996. *The "German Question" and Other German Questions*. New York: St. Martin's Press.

Schwartz, Justin. 1991. A Future for Socialism in the USSR? In *Communist Regimes – The After Math: Socialist Register 1991*. Pp. 67-94. London: Merlin Press.

Segall, M. 1983. On the Concept of a Socialist Health System: A Question of Marxist Epidemiology. *International Journal of Health Services* 13:221-225.

Sherman, Howard J. and James L. Wood. 1979. *Sociology: Traditional and Radical Perspectives*. New York; Harper & Row.

Smith, Duncan. 1988. *Walls and Mirrors: Western Representations of Really Existing Socialism in the German Democratic Republic*. Lanham, MD: University Press of America.

Sontheimer, Kurt and William Bleek. 1975. *The Government and Politics of East Germany*. London: Hutchinson University Library.

Spiegel, Der. 1995. Stolz aufs eigene Leben. No. 27, Pp. 40-52.

Stahnke, Arthur A. 1983. GDR Economic Strategy in the 1980s: The 1981-85 Plan. In *Studies in GDR Culture and Society 3*. Pp. 1-12. Margy Gerber, ed. Lanham, MD: University Press of America.

Steele, Jonathan. 1977. *Inside East Germany: The State That Came in from the Cold*. New York: Urizen Books.

Steiniger, Rolf. 1990. *The German Question: The Stalin Note of 1952 and the Problem of Reunification.* New York: Columbia University Press.

Suess, Walter. 1989 East Germany's Defensive Politics. *Telos,* No. 79:163-180.

Thomaneck, Jurgen. 1979/80. The Relationship Between the GDR and the FRG: The Origins. *GDR Monitor,* No. 2:7-14.

Torpey, John C. 1995. *Intellectuals, Socialism, and Dissent: The East German Opposition and Its Legacy.* Minneapolis: University of Minnesota Press.

US Arms Control and Disarmament Agency. 1988. *World Military Expenditures and Arms Transfers.* Washington, D.C.: US Government Printing Office.

Wallerstein, Immanuel. 1979. *The Capitalist World-Economy.* Cambridge: Cambridge University Press.

Wensierski, Peter. 1984. The New Politics of Detente Starts at the Bottom: The Unofficial Peace Movement in the GDR. *Studies in GDR Culture and Society, Vol. 4. Margy* Gerber, ed. Pp. 79-94. Lanham, MD: University Press of America.

Whetten, Lawrence L. 1980. *Germany East and West: Conflicts, Collaboration, and Confrontation.* New York: New York University Press.

Wittich, Dietmar. 1995. Mitglieder und Waehler der PDS. In *Die PDS: Empirische Befunde & Kontroverse Analysen.* Michael Brie, Martin Herzig, and Thomas Koch, eds. Pp. 58-80. Koeln: PapaRosa Verlag.

Woods, Roger. 1986. *Opposition in the GDR Under Honecker, 1971-1985.* New York: St. Martin's Press.

_____. 1993. Civil Society, Critical Intellectuals, and Public Opinion in the New Bundeslaender. In *Studies in GDR Culture and Society: The End of the GDR and the Problems of Integration.* Margy Gerber & Roger Woods, eds. Lanham, MD: University Press of America.

Index